Louis Tronson

Examination of Conscience Upon Special Subjects

Louis Tronson

Examination of Conscience Upon Special Subjects

ISBN/EAN: 9783744660136

Printed in Europe, USA, Canada, Australia, Japan

Cover: Foto ©Thomas Meinert / pixelio.de

More available books at **www.hansebooks.com**

ASCETIC LIBRARY

Vol. IV.

Examination of Conscience

RIVINGTONS

London .... *Waterloo Place*
Oxford .... *High Street*
Cambridge .... *Trinity Street*

Examination of Conscience

UPON

SPECIAL SUBJECTS

TRANSLATED AND ABRIDGED FROM THE FRENCH OF

TRONSON

EDITED BY THE

REV. ORBY SHIPLEY, M.A.

RIVINGTONS
London, Oxford, and Cambridge
1870

Advertisement.

LOUIS TRONSON, born in Paris about the year 1621, was the son of Louis Tronson, Secretary to the Privy Council under Louis the Thirteenth, by his wife Claude de Sève. Having completed his studies in Paris, he was ordained Priest, and received the appointment of Chaplain to the King. His earnest desire of exercising himself in the Ascetic Life, caused him to resign this post in 1655; and he then entered the Seminary of S. Sulpice, which had been recently founded. Here he gave so much edification by the religious zeal and discretion with which he discharged the duties of the different offices connected with the establishment, that, in the year 1676, he was chosen Superior of the Seminary, with its dependent Colleges. He wrote two works, which are highly esteemed: the "Examens Particuliers," first printed at Lyons in 1690, had been previously very widely circulated in manuscript, and several editions have subsequently appeared. His second work, entitled "Forma Cleri," is a collection of rules taken from Holy Writ, from the decrees of the Councils of the Church, and from the writings of the Fathers, for the life and conduct of the Priesthood. Only three volumes in duodecimo were issued at first; but in the year 1724 the entire work was published in quarto by the Paris press. M. Tronson engaged in the controversy which arose upon the publication of the book called "The Maxims of the Saints," by Fénélon, Archbishop of Cambrai; and he took part in the conferences at Issy, where the Articles since known as the Issy Articles were drawn up, as may be seen in the treatise on "Quietism" by Bossuet, Bishop of Meaux. He died, February the 26th, 1700, aged 79 years, held in great reverence for his deep piety. His remains were interred in the crypt of the Seminary Chapel.

* * * * *

The special Self-interrogation of Conscience, which is so earnestly counselled by the Saints of GOD, as one of the most efficacious aids to the soul desirous of making progress in the Spiritual Life, consists in a searching inquisition, not merely into our graver faults, but into our smallest failings—taking each one separately, and reviewing it with respect to the virtue which we wish to acquire, or the sin which we desire to avoid—that so we may labour the more earnestly wholly to root them out, and thus, by the Divine Grace, stand without reproach before GOD and man.

Regarding the exercise of Self-examination in this light, we may plainly see the utility and the necessity thereof; and we have only to practise it diligently for a time, to be practically convinced of the great spiritual profit which we may thence derive.

True it is that Self-examination presents many difficulties, even to those who want neither good-will nor spiritual discernment: for, whether it be that self-love renders their faults imperceptible to themselves—whether the sustained attention, which is requisite to enable them to discover their faults, be too irksome to them—or whether the mind, accustomed to indulge itself by dwelling on pleasing images, is reluctant to pursue a research so unsatisfactory to human vanity—it is certain that there are few persons to whom rigid Self-interrogation on the subject of their failings is not wearisome or repelling.

The following chapters may perhaps prove a help to those who are discouraged by such difficulties.

They will here see, briefly set before them, the various imperfections to which they are most subject, with the temptations consequent thereupon; beholding themselves, as it were, reflected in a glass, which, by making manifest their defects, enables them promptly to seek a remedy for the same.

It is also thought that those who have the Direction of souls, may here find some hints which may serve in the preparation of exhortations to their penitents.

To those, also, who practise mental prayer, this little work may be useful; for they will here see placed before them, at one view, the duty which they owe to GOD; reflections calculated to awaken them to a full conviction of the Verities upon which they meditate; the resolutions which they should endeavour to make; and the prayers which they may offer up for the fulfilment of their requests.

Each chapter lays down rules for our guidance, with reference to the subject of which it treats; gives a table of the faults most frequently committed under that particular head; and contains several exercises of piety, applicable to the circumstances of all readers.

Some chapters are more especially intended for Priests, but the greater number are equally adapted for Clerics and Laymen.

In some portions the details may be thought too minute and trivial, and it may be considered that many of the faults passed in review are mere external defects of manner: but let us remember that to the soul which truly fears and loves GOD, nothing, how unimportant soever it may appear, is a matter to be neglected; that without a strict outward rule, it is impossible to keep guard over the heart; and that it is those who pass over trifling faults, who are in most danger of falling into grievous sin. The Fathers of the Church did not despise these minute details, and we may, surely, be content to follow in their footsteps. "Who hath despised the day of small things?" (Zech. 4. 10.)

In conclusion, we can only entreat the reader to co-operate with the writer of this little work in the object proposed, which is—that we may all, by the grace of GOD, acquire a deep abhorrence of sin, a true love of virtue, and an earnest desire of making progress in the Spiritual Life, that thereby we may be enabled, with fear and trembling, to work out our salvation.

NOTE.

The present translation has been considerably abridged in substance, and wholly re-arranged in form, in order to make it more practically useful for English Churchmen. The chapters more especially intended for the Clergy have been collected into a distinct part by themselves.

Contents.

	PAGE
Of Faith.	
The gift of Faith	1
Living by Faith	4
The confession of our Faith	6
Of Hope	8
Of Trust in God	11
Of Charity.	
The Love of God	14
The contemplative Love of God	17
The active Love of God	19
Of Submission to the Divine Will	22
Of the Love which we owe our Lord Jesus Christ	24
Of the Love of our Neighbour.	
That we should love our Neighbour as ourselves	26
That we should love him with a pure Love, as Christ has loved us	28
That our Love for him should be tender and sympathizing, like the Love of our Blessed Lord for us	30
That our Love for him should be strong and constant, like the Love of our Blessed Lord	32
How we should bear with his failings	34
How closely this Love should unite all Christians	36

	PAGE
Of the Love of our Neighbour—*(continued)*.	
How we should maintain peace between our brethren	38
The true signs of this Virtue	40
Some objects contrary to this Virtue	43
The Love of our Enemies	45
Of the Christian's true Wisdom, and the Counsels thereof	47
Of Humility.	
The esteem and love we should have for this Virtue	49
Self-knowledge is the chief foundation of this Virtue	51
The First Degree of this Virtue is to esteem ourselves lowly	53
The Second Degree of this Virtue makes us rejoice when we are humbled	55
Of Pride	57
Of Vanity	59
Of Presumption and Self-Confidence	61
Of Patience.	
Patience, as a Virtue	63
Patience under special trials	65
Faults to be avoided in time of Sickness	68
The lessons taught us by Sickness	70
Of Recovery from Sickness	72
Of Sloth	74
Of Temptations.	
How we should bear ourselves when assailed by Temptation	76
Special Temptations	78
Of the Employment of our Time	81
Of the Peace of God	83
Of Christian Meekness	85

Contents.

	PAGE
Of Lukewarmness	87

Of the Examination of Conscience.
The high estimation in which this Duty should be held by us 89
The manner in which this Duty should be performed by us 91

Of Confession.
How we should prepare ourselves for this Sacrament . 94
Contrition 96
How we make confession of our Sins 98
On Satisfaction 100

Of Direction.
The needfulness thereof for all men 103
The necessity of choosing a skilful and prudent Director 105
How we should bear ourselves towards our Director . 107

Of Holy Communion.
Of preparing ourselves for Holy Communion . . 109
The acts which we should make to obtain the Grace of a worthy Communion 113
The desire which should possess us for frequent Communion 116
Thanksgiving after Communion 119
How we should dispose ourselves to assist devoutly and profitably at the Celebration of the Holy Eucharist . 122

Of Penitence.
The First Fruit of Penitence, which is Hatred of Sin . 125
The Second Fruit of Penitence, which is Self-abhorrence 127
The Third Fruit of true Penitence, which is Love of the Cross 129

	PAGE
Of Penitence—*(continued)*.	
The Fourth Fruit of Penitence, which is Peace of Heart	131
The means by which true Penitents may derive benefit even from their falls	133
The Penitential Spirit	135
Of Devotional Reading	137
Of Reading the Holy Scriptures	139
Of Hearing the Word of God worthily . . .	141
Of our Daily Duties.	
The care we should take to discharge them well .	143
The spirit in which we should discharge them .	145
The necessity of referring all we do to our Lord Jesus Christ	147
Some helps given us to enable us the better to discharge them	150
Of Mental Prayer.	
How this devout exercise should be valued and loved by us	153
How we should prepare ourselves for Meditation .	156
The Preparation: which is the First Part of the Meditation	158
The Substance: which is the Second Part of the Meditation.—First Division	161
The Substance: which is the Second Part of the Meditation.—Second Division	163
The Substance: which is the Second Part of the Meditation.—Third Division	165
The Conclusion: which is the Third Part of the Meditation	167
The benefit which we should derive from Mental Prayer	169

Contents.   xiii

                                                                    PAGE

Of Mental Prayer—(*continued*).
   *The wanderings of thought which trouble us during
     Meditation* 171
   Dryness and other trials in Mental Prayer . . . 173

Of Christian Modesty 175

Of being Poor in Spirit 177

Of our Waking and Rising 179

Of Conversation.
   The Faults which we should avoid in Conversation . 181
   The Virtues to be exercised in Conversation . . . 183

Of Travelling.
   How to use profitably the time so spent 185

Of Retreats 187

Of Self-discipline.
   The needfulness of this Virtue 189
   The exercise of this Virtue 191
   The subdual of our Evil Tempers and Natural Inclinations 193
   The discipline of the Intellect 195
   The subdual of the Love of Self 197

EXAMEN PRO CLERO.

Of the Saintliness of Life required in the Priesthood . 199
Of being called to the Priesthood 202
Of the Signs of our calling to the Priesthood . . . 204
Of the Priestly Spirit 206
Of the frame of mind in which we should receive the
   Gift of Holy Orders . , ... 209

	PAGE
Of administering the Holy Sacraments	211
Of the preparation necessary to enable Priests worthily to Celebrate	213
Of Divine Service.	
How we should prepare ourselves for conducting it	216
The frame of mind in which we should celebrate it	219
The outward demeanour with which we should celebrate it	221
Of the Ceremonies of the Church	223
Of Preaching	225
Of Catechizing	227
Of Priestly Studies.	
The high estimation in which Study should be held by us	229
The rules which we should observe in our Studies	231
Rules to enable us to pursue our Studies in a Christian spirit	233
Of Pastoral Visits	235
Of the good Example which Priests are bound to give	238
Of the Renewal of Baptismal Vows	240
Of the Spirit of the World.	
The signs of this Worldly Spirit	242
Of the warfare which Priests are bound to maintain against the World	244
Of Obedience.	
The reverence and love Priests should feel for this Virtue	246
The practice of this Virtue	248
Viri Venerabiles	250

EXAMINATION OF CONSCIENCE
UPON SPECIAL SUBJECTS

EXAMINATION OF CONSCIENCE.

Of Faith.

THE GIFT OF FAITH.

FIRST POINT.

LET us adore GOD as the Supreme Ruler of all things, and as the One and Only Source of all Truth. He, by giving us the gift of faith, and by revealing to us the wondrous mysteries of Faith, hath called us "out of darkness into His marvellous light" (1 S. Pet. ii. 9), and hath "translated us into the Kingdom of His dear SON" (Col. i. 13). What thanks, then, what praises should we not give to this GOD of Mercy, in that He hath been pleased to enrich us with the priceless treasure of Divine faith. Verily, "He hath not dealt so with any nation" (Ps. cxlvii. 20).

SECOND POINT.

LET us ask ourselves whether we have not fallen into some of the sins against this gift of faith.

Has our faith been really earnest and sincere, or have we not contented ourselves with a mere outward profession of our holy Faith? Have we firmly believed all the revealed truths of GOD, making no exception for doubt, even in the smallest particular?

Have we believed undoubtingly, without hesitating or giving heed to what our senses and our reason may have suggested? Has our belief been single-hearted—that is to say, have we believed simply because GOD has revealed these truths to His Church, whence we receive them? Have we not been amongst those who, instead of submitting humbly to the decisions of the Church, seek by subtle arguments to oppose them, or at all events to find excuses for evading such as are repugnant to our reason? Have we not also felt such overweening confidence in our own opinions as to estimate them as Articles of Faith to which the Church has given her sanction?

If we readily accept truths which are theoretical, do we not make difficulties as to those which are more practical? When we read in the Gospel that true peace in this life is to be found in poverty, in contempt of the world, and in suffering—that we must renounce self and love our enemies, have we believed these truths as fully as we believe in the existence of GOD, or in the Incarnation and Death of our LORD JESUS CHRIST?

Have we not endeavoured to search too curiously into mysteries; and, striving to expound them by the light of mere human reason, have we not exposed ourselves to numberless temptations against the Faith? Have we carefully avoided all books, conversations, and discussions, which might prove, either to ourselves or to others, a source of temptation on this point?

When we have felt any temptation concerning our faith, instead of trying to combat it by argument, have we humbled ourselves and cast ourselves at the feet of our SAVIOUR with the prayer of the Apostles, "LORD, increase our faith"? (S. Luke xvii. 5.) To become worthy of this grace, and to establish ourselves in the Faith of the Church, have we sought to strengthen others, either by making known to them the great verities of Religion, or by explaining their doubts, or, above all, by instructing children and the poor?

Lastly, have we been specially careful to make frequent acts of faith—particularly upon the truths concerning which we know ourselves to be most tempted to doubt?

The Gift of Faith.

THIRD POINT.

O MY GOD, if Thy Saints took delight in forsaking all things to preserve their faith, it was because they knew that faith was the chief stay of all Thy gifts, that it made them of the number of Thine, and that without it they could not please Thee. Grant to us, LORD, we beseech Thee, to feel this also; and fill our hearts with the same holy desires, so that, like Thy Saints of old, we may have grace to choose to die rather than to lose our faith. "We dread the death of the body less than the death of faith" (S. Bernard).

Of Faith.

LIVING BY FAITH.

FIRST POINT.

LET us adore our LORD JESUS CHRIST as the "Author and Finisher of our faith" (Heb. xii. 2). He wills that we should sanctify ourselves, and walk in His ways, and to this end He·desires that we should live by faith, and thus, in a measure, become partakers of the Divine life which He shares co-equally with His FATHER. Oh, how precious is this life of faith! What more bounden duty have we than to follow Him Who is pleased to call us thereto?

SECOND POINT.

LET us now examine ourselves, and ask:

Do we live by faith? that is to say, is faith the guiding principle of our life, the rule of our thoughts and actions, and the standard of all our conduct? Do we view all things with the eye of faith? Do we judge all things by the light of faith, and do we weigh their true value by her balance?

Are we not, rather, led away by the false notions which we imbibe in the world—despising what it contemns, and prizing what it esteems, without regard to the teaching of faith, or the unerring judgment of GOD?

And is it not from our being so lightly impressed by the precepts of this Divine virtue, that we find it hard to endure poverty, and to love humiliations and crosses; and that we long so eagerly for the riches, honours, and pleasures of this world?

In all our difficulties, perplexities, and doubts, do we seek refuge with Faith, and make her our counsellor, carefully abstaining from taking any step except upon Christian grounds?

Have we not, even in such of our actions as seem praiseworthy, been actuated chiefly by merely human motives—giving alms from a natural feeling of compassion, helping our neighbour in order to be helped by him in turn, behaving circumspectly out of regard to the opinion of others, and putting a check upon our evil inclinations, that we may appear virtuous in the eyes of the world?

Have we not even frequently performed our religious duties, not simply to please GOD, as faith would have us perform them; but rather to gratify ourselves by the sensible consolation and sweetness which we experience in fulfilling them?

In order to establish ourselves firmly in the life of faith, do we renounce the wisdom of this world, and the accommodating spirit of the age in which we live, the maxims of which are at variance with the Spirit of CHRIST?

Do we habitually nourish our souls with the Divine truths of our holy Religion, taking pleasure in meditating on them, and letting our thoughts dwell upon them, so as to be enabled by GOD'S grace to act up to them?

Lastly, are we specially careful, now that opportunity is given us, to fill our minds with the holy precepts of the Gospel—so opposed to all worldly teaching—and to take them for our rule of life; that so we may say with the Apostle, "I live by the faith of the SON of GOD"? (Gal. ii. 20.)

THIRD POINT.

O MY GOD, I know that if we follow our instincts, we lead a merely animal existence; if we obey reason only, we are guided by a false philosophy: but if we are ruled by the teaching of Faith, we live as Christians and as Thy disciples. It is this life, O GOD, which we ask of Thee, and which Thy Church beseeches for her children, that we may henceforth faithfully keep Thy Commandments, and confess Thy holy Name.

Of Faith.

THE CONFESSION OF OUR FAITH.

FIRST POINT.

LET us adore our LORD JESUS CHRIST, Who speaks thus to all His disciples: "Whosoever shall confess Me before men, him will I confess also before My FATHER Which is in Heaven" (S. Matt. x. 32). Let us give Him thanks for this comforting assurance, and, above all, for our being placed by Him in a state in which we may avail ourselves of it, since He has given us the grace of being born of Christian parents, of being brought to Him by Holy Baptism, and of being instructed in the faith of His Church.

SECOND POINT.

LET us, then, examine how we make confession of our faith, and whether we bear witness to it before GOD and man, in thought, word, and deed.

Firstly, In Thought. When we have been tempted in thought against the faith, have we inwardly testified to GOD our desire to believe without questioning, seeking no proof save in the teaching of His Word? Have we at such times offered up to Him the sacrifice of our natural reason, bowing down our human intellect under the yoke of faith? When any proposition contrary to faith has been advanced in our presence, have we taken care to offer, in reparation for the irreverence shown to GOD, an act of faith in the particular truth which has been under discussion? Have we from time to time, in accordance both with the precepts and the practice of GOD'S

Saints, renewed our Baptismal vows, promising to believe all truths revealed by GOD to His Church, and to endeavour to guide our lives by the same?

Secondly, In Word. Have we always recited the Creeds of the Church in the spirit of faith—that is to say, attentively and reverently, and with absolute belief in all the doctrines therein contained? Have we read the Holy Scriptures in the like frame of mind? Have we not, rather, been as those of whom the Apostle speaks, who are "ashamed of the Gospel of CHRIST," who "hold the Truth in unrighteousness" (Rom. i. 16. 18)—those who, from fear or false shame, dare not uphold the Christian Faith against those who assail it? Have we spoken of the world and of worldly things in the spirit of renunciation, as by our Baptismal vow we are bound to speak of them?

Thirdly, In Deed. Have we not been ashamed to profess ourselves Christians—not daring to make use of the holy Sign of the Cross, or to kneel upon our knees, or even to pray, in the presence of others? Has not human respect hindered us sometimes from visiting the poor and sick, and from performing other works of charity, instead of rejoicing, as we ought, in being permitted to show our faith by our works, as S. James instructs us that we should do? (S. James ii. 18.)

Lastly. Do we, on all fitting occasions, make manifest that we glory in being Christians consecrated to the HOLY TRINITY, and disciples of our SAVIOUR, CHRIST JESUS the LORD?

THIRD POINT.

O MY GOD, how terrible, to the soul which can realize the misery of losing Thee, is the sentence which Thou hast pronounced against those who are ashamed to confess themselves Christians. The very thought is enough to fill us with fear. O LORD, make us, we beseech Thee, to understand the wretchedness of such a state, and vouchsafe to imprint deeply in our inmost hearts these awful words, "Whosoever shall be ashamed of Me and of My words, of him shall the SON of MAN be ashamed when He shall come in His own glory" (S. Luke ix. 26).

Of Hope.

FIRST POINT.

LET us adore the infinite Goodness of our GOD, Who vouchsafes to be Himself the Object of His children's hope, and Who has promised that those who faithfully serve Him here, shall possess Him for ever hereafter. How great is the happiness of being permitted to raise our hopes so high—even to the possession of the Eternal: and how sweetly does this expectation solace us in our exile, and temper the hardness of this present life. Let us give thanks to GOD for a bounty so far exceeding our deserts.

SECOND POINT.

CHRISTIAN Hope requires that the soul, filled with a lively faith in the Power and Goodness of ALMIGHTY GOD, and resting on His promises and on the infinite Merits of our SAVIOUR CHRIST, should confidently look to possess Him in Eternity, and to receive from Him all the succour which she needs in this life, provided that she remains ever faithful to Him. Let us examine, then, whether or not we have fulfilled all the conditions which this virtue exacts from us.

Do we firmly believe that GOD wills the salvation of all men; and has our confidence never been shaken by doubts upon this point? Have we, especially, felt a sure and certain hope that the Divine grace would supply all that is wanting to ensure our salvation?

Have we not been troubled by thoughts of distrust, and by vain fears as to our acceptance—not daring to realize that our

LORD died for us, individually, and therefore imagining that we had no real foundation for our trust in the efficacy of His Merits?

In our temptations, our sorrows, and our weariness, have we not suffered ourselves to be easily discouraged, sometimes even going so far as to think that GOD has forsaken us, instead of saying, as did the holy Patriarch Job in the midst of his afflictions, "Though He slay me, yet will I trust in Him"? (Job xiii. 15.)

In such times of trial do we trust unreservedly in the Goodness of God, and in the power of His grace, remembering that His Apostle has told us that He "will not suffer" us "to be tempted above that" we "are able; but will with the temptation also make a way to escape, that" we "may be able to bear it"? (1 Cor. x. 13.)

In all our necessities, as well of the body as of the soul, do we have recourse to Him with as perfect a confidence as that which children feel towards a kind father?

When we have been so unhappy as to offend Him, instead of returning to cast ourselves at His feet, like the Prodigal Son in the parable, have we not, rather, fled from His presence like the wretched Cain after he had slain his brother?

Have we not, on the other hand, presumed too much upon His Mercy, persuading ourselves that His Goodness being infinite, we have no cause to fear His Justice; and have we not, consequently, allowed ourselves as it were to stagnate in our sins, putting off our repentance, neglecting our duties, and thus hindering the great work of our salvation?

Lastly, have we remembered that we are not only counselled, but commanded to exercise the virtue of hope?

We are, therefore, bound to make frequent acts of confidence in GOD, and more especially at such times as we are liable to temptations against this virtue.

THIRD POINT.

O MY GOD, when I remember the words of Thine Apostle, that hope is "as an anchor of the soul, both sure and steadfast" (Heb. vi. 19), and, likewise, the saying of Thy Prophet, that "the eye of the LORD is . . . . upon them that hope in His Mercy, to deliver their soul from death" (Ps. xxxiii. 18, 19), I feel how great must be the happiness of those who truly and wholly hope in Thee, and I most earnestly desire to be of their number. May Thy Blessing, O LORD, be upon this my desire, that so, whatever chances and changes may await me in this mortal life, my soul may ever remain firmly anchored in Thee, and that thus I may be enabled to experience the truth of these words of the Son of Sirach, "Did ever any trust in the LORD and was confounded?" (Ecclus. ii. 10.)

Of Trust in God.

FIRST POINT.

LET us adore the All-merciful GOD, Who with fatherly tenderness inviteth us to put our whole trust in Him. "Cast thy burden upon the LORD, and He shall sustain thee" (Ps. lv. 22). He knows that our perils are great, and that our enemies are very powerful; and in order to deliver us from the one, and to shield us from the other, He vouchsafes to be Himself our Strength, our Hope, and our Refuge. "Thou hast been a Shelter for me, and a strong Tower from the enemy" (Ps. lxi. 3). Let us humbly render our thanks and praises to the Divine Giver of all good gifts.

SECOND POINT.

LET us ask ourselves, whether we have that entire trust in GOD which He requires of us, and which it is our bounden duty to feel. He who is firmly grounded in this virtue, rests wholly, both for his present and his future, upon the Goodness of his Heavenly FATHER. He counts as nothing the patronage of monarchs, the favour of the great ones of this world, or of any human being, for he knows that all are alike but instruments in the hand of GOD; and, therefore, whether their support be given or withdrawn, he is neither elated nor cast down thereby. He is not disquieted, even though he finds himself forsaken by those nearest and dearest to him; and, though the whole world should rise up against him, he would still possess his soul in perfect peace, saying with the kingly Prophet, "The LORD is my light and my salvation; whom then shall I fear?" (Ps. xxvii. 1.) If he is appointed to any post, he does not refuse it from fear that his health and strength may fail, or that he may be wanting in the necessary qualifications; for he knows that GOD never abandons His children in the time of need, and that when it so pleases Him, He can make use of the humblest of His servants for the increase of His glory. He is not greatly troubled if his worldly affairs are unprosperous, for he is assured that those who serve GOD faithfully shall receive all that is needful for them; and should he be tempted to subtract any portion of his time from the service of GOD in order to provide for his subsistence, he remembers the maxim of the Holy Gospel: "Take therefore no thought for the morrow; for the morrow shall take thought for the things of itself" (S. Matt. vi. 34). Thus he does not fret himself concerning the future; but relies wholly upon the Almighty FATHER, Who knows each want of His creatures. In all his undertakings, in his worldly occupations, and in the whole ordering of his life, he places no dependence on his birth, wealth, education, or talents; but, whilst acting with as much prudence and energy as though success could be obtained by his own efforts, he acknowledges that it is GOD alone Who giveth the increase. He does not even lean too much upon the spiritual privileges which he enjoys; and, although he may find the guidance of his Director to be very profitable, and particular devotions to be extremely helpful, or solitude to be almost essential to the health of his soul, yet, should none of these be attainable, he remains in great peace, consoled by the reflection that he is deprived of them by GOD'S holy Will. In sickness, bereavement, or any other calamity, he seeks for comfort and support from GOD alone, in Whom only can help be found. Lastly, whatever may be his needs, corporal or spiritual, whatever may be his sorrows, personal or for others, he strives to follow the example of the Patriarch, who, having trusted GOD wholly in the midst of his bitterest trials, was rewarded by the fulness of the Divine Blessing. Let us examine whether such has been our frame of mind.

THIRD POINT.

O MY GOD, I know that Thou dost delight in those souls who

put their trust in Thee, and Thou dost pour Thy blessings upon them most abundantly; Thou hast said, too, by Thy Prophet, " Cursed be the man that trusteth in man, and maketh flesh his arm" (Jer. xvii. 5). Can I then, knowing this, wilfully draw down upon myself the reproach addressed to "the man that made not GOD his strength, but trusted in the abundance of his riches, and strengthened himself in his wickedness"? (Ps. lii. 7.) Give me Thy grace, O LORD, that henceforth I may cast myself upon Thee alone, instead of clinging to creatures who are erring and feeble as myself, and of whom S. Augustine saith, "Subject themselves to death, they slay those who trust in them."

Of Charity.

THE LOVE OF GOD.

FIRST POINT.

LET us adore GOD, Who giveth to man the sweet commandment of love, "Thou shalt love the LORD thy GOD" (Deut. vi. 5. S. Mark xii. 30). The All-perfect and Supreme Being needs not our love; yet He vouchsafes to require it of us. The Angels love Him: those blessed Spirits are wholly absorbed in His love. The Seraphim, who stand nearest to His Throne, burn with the celestial flame of Divine love: yet He permits earth to share in the Bliss of Heaven by uniting both in the bond of the love of Him. He not only permits this, but He commands it—nay, did we fail to pay this tribute of love we should incur His displeasure. Let us with reverent wonder contemplate the fathomless depths of the Divine love, and let us repeat with S. Augustine, "What am I, O LORD, in Thy sight, that my love should be pleasing to Thee, or that my want of love should be grievous to Thee?"

SECOND POINT.

CHARITY commands us to give to GOD a pure love, a love exceeding all things—to love Him with all our heart, with all our mind, with all our soul, and with all our strength. Let us now see whether we have loved Him thus.

Firstly. Have we given Him a *pure* love: that is to say, have we loved Him for Himself alone, because He is infinitely Good and infinitely Perfect, and because all the love which we can give Him is but His due? When we have felt moved to love Him because of His infinite Goodness, has it not been rather on account of His goodness to ourselves, because He has given us great earthly blessings, or because we hope for the reward which He has promised hereafter to those who love Him? Have we taken care to make from time to time acts of the pure love of GOD? When we have told Him that we love Him solely for Himself, are we not satisfied with the mere phrase, instead of seeking to kindle the feeling in our hearts?

Secondly. Have we loved Him *above all things*—more than all the goods of this world, more than all creatures, more than ourselves? Do we esteem the glory of belonging to Him, of serving Him and pleasing Him, as being far beyond all the riches, the honours, and the pleasures of this world? Are we willing to renounce our dearest affections and friendships, rather than to be unfaithful to GOD? Are we ready to sacrifice our will, our health, our life, rather than to risk His displeasure or the loss of His grace?

Thirdly. Have we loved Him with *all our heart*—not halving our love, but loving Him before all, and above all, and all things in Him and for Him?

Fourthly. Do we love Him with *all our mind*—delighting in meditating upon Him, and upon the best method of corresponding with His designs in our behalf?

Fifthly. Do we love Him with *all our soul*—submitting all our powers and senses to Him, and employing them wholly in serving Him and in promoting His Glory?

Sixthly. Do we love Him with *all our strength*—joyfully spending it in His cause, and never sparing ourselves when we have any work to do for Him?

Lastly. Have we given ourselves up to the guidance of the HOLY SPIRIT, beseeching Him to write the law of Love in our hearts, that so His grace may enable us to fulfil, with the utmost perfection, this "the first and great Commandment"? (S. Matt. xxii. 38.)

THIRD POINT.

O MY GOD, Thou art All-loving, and Thou dost desire that I should give Thee my heart. Thou dost shower down gifts upon me, Thou dost overshadow me with the wings of Thy love, and yet, even now, I hardly know how to love Thee as I ought. How great is my shame and confusion when I reflect upon my own hardness and insensibility. O LORD, grant me, I pray Thee, the grace which S. Augustine demanded of Thee when he prayed thus: "O Fire, ever burning and never quenched: O Love, ever fervent and never growing cold: Enkindle in me Thy light, and draw me wholly to Thee, that I may in all things become pleasing to Thee!"

Of Charity.

THE CONTEMPLATIVE LOVE OF GOD.

FIRST POINT.

LET us adore our Blessed SAVIOUR, contemplating with joyful love the Infinite and unspeakable Perfections of His Heavenly FATHER. They are the constant subject of His thoughts. He speaks continually of them to His people, and in all things He shows how entirely the contemplative Love of the Divine Majesty possesses Him. Let us give thanks to our dear LORD for thus glorifying His FATHER by the purity of His Love, and for obtaining for us the grace whereby we may follow His Example.

SECOND POINT.

THE soul which is filled with the contemplative love of GOD has no greater joy than in meditating upon Him. When she considers His Greatness, His Omnipotence, and all His other Attributes, she loses herself in the abyss of contemplation, and in so losing herself finds her most perfect rest. She is so ravished with the sight of the All-perfect Beauty revealed to her by the eye of faith, that all earthly joys are to her vain and empty, whilst the Divine Love alone is steadfast and immovable. She only desires that which GOD willeth: she loves what He loveth: that alone which is displeasing to Him is hateful to her. So entirely is her heart in conformity with GOD'S holy Will, that she longs far more ardently that It should be accomplished than that any desire of her own should be fulfilled. Thus does she dwell always in perfect peace, abandoning herself wholly to GOD, and submitting joyfully to whatever His Providence may appoint. Sickness or health, poverty or riches, life or death, are equally welcome to her, for she knows that her Beloved is from everlasting, and that none of His promises shall fail. She rejoices with a holy joy, when she pictures to herself the perpetual Sacrifice of prayer and praise in which the Church Militant and the Church Triumphant join, and which is presented to the FATHER by the Beloved SON, Who alone can meetly honour Him. Lastly, so great is her delight in the contemplation of the Divine Perfection, that she would willingly repeat without ceasing the words to which the great multitude, in the Apocalyptic Vision, give utterance before the throne: " Blessing, and glory, and wisdom, and thanksgiving, and honour, and power, and might, be unto our GOD for ever and ever. Amen" (Rev. vii. 12). Let us now see whether we have been in this devout frame of mind, which is essential to the contemplative love of GOD.

THIRD POINT.

O MY GOD, how happy is the soul which loves Thee purely and entirely, and whose greatest joy is to know Thee, All-perfect as Thou art. To her has been revealed that great mystery of dying to all created things and of living to Thee alone, in which consists the blessedness of the redeemed in Heaven. I offer to Thee, O LORD, my earnest desire to be filled with this Divine Love. Possess my heart with it, I beseech Thee, that thus I may experience the truth of those words of S. Augustine, " He is beloved by GOD to whom GOD is All in all."

Of Charity.

THE ACTIVE LOVE OF GOD.

FIRST POINT.

LET us adore our LORD JESUS CHRIST, Who throughout His Life on earth never ceased to manifest His active Love towards His Heavenly FATHER. Since the glory which the ALMIGHTY concentrated in Himself from all eternity admitted of no increase, the Divine SON laboured earnestly to magnify Him throughout time amongst His Creatures. Our Blessed SAVIOUR came to us, taking upon Himself the form of a servant, to reveal His FATHER to lost man, and to establish His Kingdom on earth. To accomplish this He shed the last drop of His Blood, and He was ready to suffer yet more, had such been His FATHER'S Will. Let us then reverently meditate upon the active Love shown by our Divine LORD, and let us give thanks to Him for affording us so great an Example for our imitation.

SECOND POINT.

THE active love of GOD gives to the soul which is filled therewith an unceasing and ardent desire that He should be known, loved, and served by all His children, and that His Name should be exalted throughout the earth. This desire nothing can weaken in her—neither the pressure of her worldly affairs nor of her daily work; for all these things she uses profitably, and seeks therein opportunities of imparting to others the knowledge whereby they may be made wise unto salvation, and may be brought to praise GOD for ever and ever. In the ardour of her zeal she longs to see His reign established through the whole world. Far from clinging to wealth, reputation, earthly happiness, or life, she willingly risks all these, should her Master's service require such sacrifice. She cares also very earnestly for all the outward Ritual of Divine Worship, knowing that reverence for spiritual things is instilled thereby, and the Name of GOD is magnified amongst His people; and therefore she is watchful to maintain the beauty and splendour of His House, and to lavish riches upon the Altar and its sacred Vessels. She does all in her power to secure the reverent administration and participation of the Holy Sacraments, the diligent celebration of the Divine Office, and the decent ordering of all things appertaining to the Services of the Church of CHRIST. So jealous is she for the honour and glory of GOD, that it becomes a source of intense grief to her that the world should so continually disobey and offend Him. The smallest infraction of His Law gives her pain, and she offers to Him constantly acts of love, humility, and contrition, in reparation for these insults. She is willing to suffer whatever crosses may be appointed for her, and to endure them joyfully, if she may thereby contribute to the glory of GOD. Lastly, feeling that, by reason of her own weakness, she is unable to praise GOD as she ought, she calls upon all created things to join together in magnifying Him, saying from her heart with the Three Children, and with the Psalmist, "O all ye Works of the LORD, bless ye the LORD; praise and exalt Him above all for ever" (Song of the Three Children, 35). "O praise the LORD with me, and let us magnify His Name together" (Ps. xxxiv. 3). Let us now examine whether, instead of being in this frame of mind, we have not, rather, been wanting altogether in zeal for the glory of GOD; and whether the fear of receiving some trifling mortification, of undergoing some slight suffering, or of losing some temporal advantage, has not frequently made us prefer our own interests to the honour of our Master?

THIRD POINT.

O MY GOD, Who hast loved us so much as to give Thyself to us after having given us all that we possess, how can I show my gratitude for a love so boundless? I know, O LORD, what I will do. Love can be repaid only by love; therefore, by the aid of Thy grace, I will henceforth dedicate my life to Thee alone, and consume it wholly as a burnt-offering in Thy service: thus, as S. Bernard saith, " Let us, being loved, love in return, and, by loving, become worthy of being more entirely loved."

Of Submission to the Divine Will.

FIRST POINT.

LET us adore our LORD and SAVIOUR JESUS CHRIST, Who during His mortal Life, and more especially as the hour of His Passion drew nigh, showed the most perfect submission to His FATHER'S Will. He tasted by anticipation the full bitterness of the bodily torments and the mental sufferings which He was called upon to endure; yet, although His Human Nature shrank from the trial, He yet gave Himself up in loving obedience to the Divine Will, thereby setting before us a most perfect and precious Example of submission.

SECOND POINT.

LET us examine whether we have, under all circumstances, conformed ourselves perfectly to the Divine Will.

Have we not desired some position in life, or some employment, other than that ordained for us by the Providence of GOD?

Should we not have preferred choosing our station in life or our work in accordance with our own inclinations?

Have we been satisfied with the talents allotted to us by the Divine Goodness, instead of murmuring because we have received a smaller portion than has been given to others? Have we been perfectly contented with our worldly condition, remembering that it, also, has been appointed for us by Almighty GOD?

Do we receive all sorrows and privations as from the Hand of GOD; and, instead of brooding morbidly over them, do we remember that they are sent to us as a means of trial and of sanctification?

When we meditate upon death, and when we find it approaching, do we resign ourselves to it with entire trust in the Divine Mercy? Do we receive with the same spirit of resignation all public calamities, such as War, Pestilence, Famine, and unfavourable Seasons: acknowledging that all things are ordained by GOD in the secret councils of His Wisdom, and that He is able, at His pleasure, to draw good out of what appears to us the greatest evil?

Have we not desired spiritual gifts too eagerly, so as to be cast down and discouraged should GOD see fit to deprive us of them?

Lastly, have we given thanks alike in adversity and in prosperity, in joy and in sorrow, whether we are left desolate or are overwhelmed with consolations; and have we cast ourselves upon GOD for time and for eternity?

THIRD POINT.

O MY GOD, since it is certain that nothing can happen in this world save by Thy permission, and that, as the Wise Man saith, "Prosperity and adversity, life and death, poverty and riches, come of the LORD" (Ecclus. xi. 14), it is therefore our bounden duty to submit ourselves lovingly and reverently to receive from Thy hand whatever Thou hast appointed for us. This, O LORD, I am resolved to do, by the help of Thy Divine grace. May it enable me to say with S. Augustine, quoting the words of the Psalmist, "O GOD, my heart is fixed" (Ps. cviii. 1), "my heart is fixed upon Thee in prosperity, it is stayed upon Thee also in adversity."

Of the Love which we owe to our Lord Jesus Christ.

FIRST POINT.

LET us adore our LORD JESUS CHRIST, resplendent with the Glory of the FATHER, and possessing the fulness of all His Treasures. Who can depict the beauty of the Divine SAVIOUR, the Beloved, the Chosen One amongst thousands? His Heavenly FATHER delighteth in Him: should He not then be to us the sole Object of our love? He is our *Father*, our *Redeemer*, our *Master*, our *Leader*, our *All*. Let us then love Him and redouble our love for Him even to the utmost of our powers.

SECOND POINT.

LET us ask ourselves whether we have felt for our Blessed LORD all the love which is His due.

Have we loved Him as GOD made Man—above all things, more than all created things, and more than ourselves?

Do we take delight in reflecting that He is indeed the Very, Living GOD, and is it to us a source of joyful wonder to meditate upon His Greatness and His manifold Perfections?

Have we loved Him as our *Redeemer*—holding ourselves in readiness to do or to suffer whatever may be appointed to us, in a spirit of reverent gratitude for all which He did and suffered for our salvation?

Have we loved Him as our Sovereign LORD—bearing ourselves towards Him with the obedience of servants, the faithfulness of subjects, the entire dependence of vassals; and feeling joy in the thought of His supreme dominion over us?

Have we loved Him as our *Master*—receiving His teaching

with meekness, joyfully conforming ourselves to His precepts, upholding His doctrine, and earnestly desiring that His Gospel should be spread abroad through all the earth?

Have we loved Him as our *Captain* and *Leader*—being ever prepared to lay down our lives for the promoting of His Glory, as soldiers who willingly confront death for the honour of their Commander?

Have we loved Him as our *Shepherd* Who nourisheth us with His Own Blood, and have we gladly hearkened to His voice and followed Him, instead of straying from Him in search of other pastures?

Have we loved Him as our *Father*—with a reverent and trusting love, and fearing nothing save His displeasure?

Have we loved Him as the Chosen Spouse of our souls—having no other interests but His, desiring only the accomplishment of His Will, and placing our whole happiness both for time and eternity in a close and inviolable union with Him?

Lastly, have we loved Him as our *All*—"giving," as S. Bernard saith, "our whole hearts to Him Who gave Himself wholly to us"?

THIRD POINT.

WHEN I contemplate, O my JESUS, Thy countless claims upon my love; when I remember that Thou dost Thyself condescend to ask my love[1], and that Thou dost pour forth Thy graces and blessings upon those who love Thee; how must I lament the coldness which has hitherto made me insensible to so many proofs of Thy Fatherly tenderness. O LORD, I beseech Thee to kindle in my heart the love of Thee, that thus I may never be so unhappy as to fall under the sentence pronounced by Thine Apostle against those who love Thee not: "If any man love not the LORD JESUS CHRIST, let him be Anathema Maran-atha" (1 Cor. xvi. 22).

---

[1] "Behold, I stand at the door, and knock: if any man hear My voice, and open the door, I will come in to him, and will sup with him, and he with Me" (Rev. iii. 20).

Of the Love of our Neighbour.

THAT WE SHOULD LOVE OUR NEIGHBOUR AS OURSELVES.

FIRST POINT.

LET us adore the infinite Wisdom of GOD which shines forth most especially in His command to us that we should love our neighbour as ourselves. He knows how priceless are the benefits which this love will confer upon us: and as He also knows that the flesh and the Devil will exert their utmost power to destroy, or, at least, to weaken this love in us, He not only makes it the subject of an express command, but He gives us a rule whereby to gauge it, viz. that it should equal our love for ourselves; "Thou shalt love thy neighbour as thyself." Let us render humble thanks to Him from Whom all goodness and all love proceed.

SECOND POINT.

LET us examine whether we have in truth loved our neighbour as ourselves.

Have we entered as thoroughly into all which concerns him as we do into our own affairs?

Do we rejoice at any good which befalls him as heartily as though it happened to ourselves; and do we feel his sorrows as our own?

Do we seek opportunities of serving and helping him; and do we try to forestall his wishes?

In whatever intercourse we have with him, whether in society or in business, do we bear ourselves towards him with Christian humility and courtesy?

Are we careful to avoid all topics of conversation which may be disagreeable to him?

Are we as tender of his reputation as of our own?

Do we as far as is possible, consistently with our duty, endeavour to conceal his faults, to excuse them, and to change the conversation, should it turn upon such a subject?

Have we his salvation at heart; do we pray for it earnestly; and do we contemplate with joy the graces which he receives, and the faithfulness wherewith he profits by them?

Lastly, have we followed the two great rules laid down in Holy Scripture: "Thou shalt love thy neighbour as thyself" (Levit. xix. 18); and, "As ye would that men should do to you, do ye also to them likewise"? (S. Luke vi. 31.)

THIRD POINT.

O MY GOD, how perfectly is the love which Thou willest that we should bear one to another described in the record which we find in the Sacred Volume of the love of Jonathan for David. "The soul of Jonathan was knit with the soul of David, and Jonathan loved him as his own soul" (1 Sam. xviii. 1). It is thus, O LORD, that we desire henceforth to love our neighbour. We humbly beg of Thee to enable us by Thine Allpowerful Grace so to do. We ask this of Thee in the name of the great Love wherewith Thou hast loved us.

Of the Love of our Neighbour.

THAT WE SHOULD LOVE HIM WITH A PURE LOVE, AS CHRIST HAS LOVED US.

FIRST POINT

LET us adore our LORD and SAVIOUR CHRIST, Who holds before us as a model of the love which we should bear to our neighbour, the pure and perfect Love wherewith He has loved us. "A new commandment I give unto you, That ye love one another: as I have loved you, that ye also love one another" (S. John xiii. 34). He calls this commandment "a new commandment," for new it surely was in the unexampled purity, tenderness, and strength of the love which He bore to all men, and which He desired them to exercise henceforth towards each other. What grateful praises are due from us to the Divine Master Who has given us this precept of brotherly love.

SECOND POINT.

LET us now ask ourselves whether our love for our neighbour has been CHRIST-like in purity and freedom from self-seeking.

Our LORD loved us unselfishly, desiring only our salvation and His FATHER'S Glory; has our love for our neighbour, however feebly, resembled this?

Firstly. Have we not loved him from interested motives—only helping him, striving to please him, and showing him kindness and affection, when we thought that it would be to our advantage to do so? Have we not on this account pretended to approve whatever he did, however undeserving of praise we really thought him?

Secondly. Has our love for our neighbour sprung chiefly from the desire of helping him, by the Divine Grace, to work out his salvation; and has our most fervent hope been that he might give himself wholly to GOD, and that he might diligently strive to advance in the way of perfection?

Thirdly. Have we loved him in, and for, GOD, without regard to his talents, his disposition, his rank, his outward accomplishments, or to the congeniality of mind and character which may exist between ourselves and him—loving him in the spirit of Faith, because he is made in GOD'S Image, being a member of CHRIST, and a temple of the HOLY GHOST, and a child of the Church of GOD—and loving him thus, because GOD has commanded us so to do? "This is My Commandment, that ye love one another, as I have loved you" (S. John xv. 12).

THIRD POINT.

O MY GOD, I know how often I have been wanting in love of my neighbour, and this because I have not loved him with a pure unselfish affection. Grant, O LORD, that henceforth I may love him only with a view to his salvation and to Thy glory; for thus alone can my love for him be without excess and free from peril; unabsorbing yet unchangeable and wholly purified from personal feelings; in a word, "with CHRIST in GOD" (Col. iii. 3).

Of the Love of our Neighbour.

THAT OUR LOVE FOR HIM SHOULD BE TENDER AND SYMPATHIZING, LIKE THE LOVE OF OUR BLESSED LORD FOR US.

FIRST POINT.

LET us lovingly and reverently contemplate the tender and compassionate love wherewith our Blessed SAVIOUR has loved all men. He left His Throne of everlasting glory, and came amongst us that He might give us free access to His Presence. He made Himself like unto us, and was subject to all the infirmities of our nature, sin only excepted, in order that He might comfort us in all our sorrows by His full and entire participation in all that we suffer. "We have not an High Priest which cannot be touched with the feeling of our infirmities; but was in all points tempted like as we are, yet without sin" (Heb. iv. 15). Let us adore the Divine Redeemer Who is thus pitiful to us, and Who commands us to deal with our neighbour in like manner.

SECOND POINT.

LET us examine how we have endeavoured to imitate our Blessed LORD'S tender and compassionate love towards our fellow-creatures.

Have we, then, sympathized with them in all their necessities and afflictions; showing ourselves ever ready, like the Apostle, to "weep with them that weep," and striving by all means in our power to console them under their trials?

When our neighbour comes to us for advice or assistance, do

That our Love for him should be tender.

we receive him kindly and cordially, so as to convince him of the reality of our brotherly love?

Have we not, rather, repelled him by a cold and distant demeanour?

Have we given free access to all who seek us, especially to the poor; and do we earnestly strive to carry out the precept of S. Paul—that in all things we should "please" our "neighbour for his good"? (Rom. xv. 2.) In speaking to persons over whom we are placed in authority, have we not assumed a harsh, imperious manner, more resembling that of a master issuing orders to a servant, than that of one Christian addressing another?

In dealing with persons living in habitual sin, or with such as are beset with temptations, scruples, or other spiritual diseases, do we display all that tenderness, mildness, and charity which are needed to solace those who are thus grievously afflicted?

Lastly, do we lay aside all our imaginary self-importance and our pride, in order to become, as S. Paul saith, "all things to all men," that we may, in our several degrees, "by all means save some"? (1 Cor. ix. 22.)

THIRD POINT.

O MY GOD, when I remember the great Example which Thou dost give me of that tender and compassionate love which Thou commandest me to show to my neighbour; and when I recall Thy saying, "With the same measure that ye mete withal, it shall be measured to you again" (S. Luke vi. 38), how can I, wretched that I am, who myself so greatly need Thy Mercy be wanting in tender pity to my fellow-men? Grant, O LORD, I beseech Thee, that, from this time forward, in all my dealings with my neighbour, I may ever follow the rule of Thine Apostle, "Put on therefore, as the elect of GOD, ... bowels of mercies, kindness, humbleness of mind, meekness, long-suffering" (Col. iii. 12).

Of the Love of our Neighbour.

THAT OUR LOVE FOR HIM SHOULD BE STRONG AND CONSTANT, LIKE THE LOVE OF OUR DIVINE LORD.

FIRST POINT.

LET us reverently contemplate the strength of that Love which caused our Blessed LORD to suffer and to die for us. After having endured shame and grief, and the bitterest torments, He died a cruel and ignominious death, shedding the last drop of His most precious Blood; and all this was for our sakes, all this could not quench His love for us. "Many waters cannot quench love, neither can the floods drown it" (Solomon's Song, viii. 7). Who then can refrain from striving to make some return of humble thanks, and praises for so great a Love?

SECOND POINT.

LET us ask ourselves whether we have loved our neighbour with a strong, enduring love, like the Love of our LORD JESUS CHRIST.

Have we not been quickly discouraged by the most trifling obstacles which we may have encountered in our efforts to serve our neighbour? Have we not hung back and, upon the first check, relinquished our intention of assisting him?

When we try to help him, do we not do so in a cold, indifferent way, thinking more of saving ourselves trouble than of doing him service?

Have we heartily, and with good-will, risked our possessions, our health, or our life, in the cause of our neighbour?

When we visit him in sickness, do we go to him fearlessly, with a determination to overcome any feeling of repugnance, which the nature of the malady, or the condition of the patient, may excite in us?

Do we not sometimes shrink from relieving our neighbour's poverty, owing to our attachment to our worldly goods, and our consequent reluctance to part with them?

Has not the fear of ridicule led us to stifle the inspirations of the Divine Grace which urge us to instruct the ignorant, to console the sorrowful, to visit prisoners, and to tend the sick?

Lastly, have we not, through our sloth and self-indulgence, thrown away numberless opportunities of showing our love to our neighbour—most unlike in this to the Apostle S. Paul, who joyfully devoted all his powers of soul and body to the service of his fellow-creatures, without thought of return? "I will very gladly spend and be spent for you: though the more abundantly I love you, the less I be loved" (2 Cor. xii. 15).

THIRD POINT.

O MY GOD, Who didst give Thy Life for us to show us thereby the strength of Thy Love; we humbly beg of Thee the grace of which we stand in need to enable us to follow in Thy steps, and to devote all that we have, and our whole being, to the service of our neighbour. "Hereby perceive we the Love of GOD, because He laid down His Life for us, and we ought to lay down our lives for the brethren" (1 S. John iii. 16).

Of the Love of our Neighbour.

HOW WE SHOULD BEAR WITH HIS FAILINGS.

FIRST POINT.

LET us contemplate, with admiring reverence, our Blessed SAVIOUR'S loving Patience in bearing with the defects and the shortcomings of those by whom He was surrounded : and let us with grateful wonder reflect upon His great Goodness in enduring our own grievous failings. Let us give thanks for the great Love which He hereby shows us, and for the perfect Example of brotherly charity which He thus gives us. "If GOD so loved us, we ought also to love one another" (1 S. John iv. 11).

SECOND POINT.

LET us ask ourselves how we bear with our neighbour's failings.

Do we exercise all that forbearance, with respect to his faults, which we look for on behalf of our own defects?

Have we not allowed ourselves to be too much annoyed by his failings, and has not our vexation induced us to avoid his society?

Have we tried to overcome any dislike, of which we may be conscious, of the disposition or the manner of our neighbour?

Instead of trying to conceal and excuse his faults, and to bear ourselves towards him as though we were unconscious of them, have we not taken him to task in the presence of others, thus holding him up to ridicule, and making him an object of general censure?

Have we ever mocked, or taken advantage of, his bodily or

mental infirmities, his want of knowledge of the world, or his defective education?

Have we not thought it an irksome task when we have been called upon to comfort our neighbour in his affliction, to assist him in sickness, or to relieve his mental perplexities?

Lastly, have we resolved, with the help of GOD'S Grace, to comply invariably with the great rule which the Apostle has laid down for mutual forbearance, which he calls the Law of our Blessed SAVIOUR: "Bear ye one another's burdens, and so fulfil the Law of CHRIST"? (Gal. vi. 2.)

THIRD POINT.

O MOST Merciful GOD, Who hast borne with me for so long a time, I have indeed great reason to fear lest I, who am so hard and impatient with others, should thus become unworthy of Thine All-enduring Love. Pardon, I beseech Thee, my unlovingness and my want of charity. Aided by Thy Grace, I will from this time forth determine to show forbearance towards the faults of my neighbour, how painful and difficult soever this may prove : thus shall I follow the counsel of Thine Apostle : "We . . . ought to bear the infirmities of the weak, and not to please ourselves" (Rom. xv. 1).

Of the Love of our Neighbour.

HOW CLOSELY THIS LOVE SHOULD UNITE ALL CHRISTIANS.

FIRST POINT.

LET us adore the wondrous and all-perfect Unity which has subsisted throughout Eternity between the Almighty FATHER and His Divine SON : " I and My FATHER are One " (S. John x. 30). Although each Person is distinct, They form essentially but ONE—having but One Will and One Mind always operating to the same end, as the Love whose Source is in Both has but one and the same object. And even such is the union which our Blessed LORD would fain behold existing amongst Christians : " As Thou, FATHER, art in Me, and I in Thee, that they also may be one in Us " (S. John xvii. 21).

SECOND POINT.

LET us ask ourselves whether we have lived in perfect unity with our neighbour.

Is the neighbourly union which exists between us so entire that of us it may with truth be said, as of the first Christians, that there is but one heart and one soul amongst us? (Acts iv. 32.) In order to ensure, as far as in us lies, this perfect union, have we endeavoured to conform our mind and thoughts to those of our neighbour, entering into his views, listening to his arguments, and assimilating our ideas to his, so far as we can without acting against our conscience ?

Have we not been so obstinately bent on maintaining our own opinions as to try to force them upon others ?

Has not this self-opinionated spirit caused us to waste much of our time in useless disputes, and to lose our temper in defending our own side of the question, regardless of its truth or falsehood?

When we are called upon by GOD to associate in any work with others, do we strive to act in concert with them; and do we put ourselves under their direction instead of desiring to take the lead ourselves?

Lastly, have we not given way to a spirit of contradiction, leading us to despise and censure others for whatever they do or leave undone?

THIRD POINT.

O MY GOD, in order that we may henceforward live in unbroken unity with our neighbour, we beseech Thee to grant us the grace which we need to enable us to acquire those virtues of charity, meekness, courteousness, humility, and unselfishness, which Thine Apostle sets before us as the means whereby we may attain to this pure and perfect union: "Fulfil ye my joy, that ye be like-minded, having the same love, being of one accord, of one mind. Let nothing be done through strife or vainglory; but in lowliness of mind let each esteem other better than themselves" (Phil. ii. 2, 3).

Of the Love of our Neighbour.

HOW WE SHOULD MAINTAIN PEACE BETWEEN OUR BRETHREN.

FIRST POINT.

LET us adore in our LORD JESUS CHRIST the Attribute which the Apostle ascribes to Him of being "Our Peace, Who hath made both one" (Eph. ii. 14). It is He Who knits together those who appear to be most hopelessly sundered, Who unites the heavenly host to sinful man, Who joins the Jew with the Gentile, and Who causes the bitterest and most deeply-rooted enmities to cease. He is our KING, Who will have no strife or rancour in His dominion; for He is "The Prince of Peace" (Isa. ix. 6). He is our FATHER, and He will have nothing but concord between the members of His Family. "He maketh men of one manner to dwell together" (Ps. lxvii. 7, Vulg.); or, as the original has it, "after one manner," i. e. *unanimously*. He is our HEAD, and He will suffer no division amongst the Members of His Body: "We have many members in one body . . . . and are every one members one of another" (Rom. xii. 4, 5).

SECOND POINT.

LET us examine whether we endeavour to maintain unity, as far as possible, amongst our brethren.

When we observe any coolness between them, do we try to bring about a reconciliation, and do we specially apply ourselves to find out the best means of effecting this end?

When they confide to us any cause of complaint which they may have against each other, do we strive to allay their suspicions, to soften their irritated feelings, and to heal their dissensions?

Instead of seizing upon the happy opportunity which their confidence affords us of mediating between them and their opponents, have we not, either by our silence or by our apparent sympathy with their grievances, helped to increase the ill-will already existing?

Have we ever been so unhappy as to sow the seeds of discord between brethren—which in the Eye of GOD is a great and abhorrent sin? (Prov. vi. 19.)

Has not our thoughtlessness and love of gossip led us to become tale-bearers, and thus perhaps to cause serious ruptures between brethren?

When such has, unhappily, been the case, have we endeavoured promptly to atone for our sin, and have we felt a hearty contrition for it?

Have we not given bad example to others by our proneness to take offence, and by our reluctance to meet any advance towards reconciliation?

Lastly, have we, as true Children of GOD, so loved peace, that not satisfied with possessing it ourselves, we have earnestly striven to diffuse its benign influence every where and over all? "Blessed are the peacemakers; for they shall be called the Children of GOD" (S. Matt. v. 9).

THIRD POINT.

O GOD, Who art not the GOD of contention, but of peace; Thou Who art called by Thy Saints the Lover and Author of Peace, give us, we beseech Thee, some portion of this Heavenly virtue; that so we, loving peace above all things, keeping it ever in our hearts, and striving to maintain it with all mankind, may be made worthy to receive the blessing promised by Thine Apostle: "Live in peace; and the GOD of Love and Peace shall be with you" (2 Cor. xiii. 11).

Of the Love of our Neighbour.

THE TRUE SIGNS OF THIS VIRTUE.

FIRST POINT.

LET us adore our LORD JESUS CHRIST constantly inculcating the precept of the love of our neighbour. In Himself He gives us the most perfect example of it: by the mouths of the Beloved Disciple, of the other Evangelists, and of the Apostles, He again and again enforces it: throughout the Holy Gospel no duty is more repeatedly set before us. Does not this show how earnestly He desires that brotherly love should reign in our hearts, and that our actions should prove it to be sincere? Let us return our humble thanks to Him for giving us in this one Commandment the means whereby we may fulfil all our other obligations; "He that loveth another hath fulfilled the law" (Rom. xiii. 8).

SECOND POINT.

LET us now see whether we display the true signs of charity as depicted by the Apostle S. Paul in 1 Cor. xiii. True Charity "suffereth long;" bearing and forbearing, and enduring uncomplainingly the caprices, weaknesses, and defects of others. Charity "is kind;" never speaking harshly, coldly, or bitterly, and always striving to accommodate herself to the various dispositions with which she may be brought in contact. Charity "envieth not;" far from grudging the happiness or success of others, she rejoices as sincerely in their good fortune as though it were her own. Charity "doth not behave itself unseemly;" she does not act from the whim or the temper of the moment;

she never feigns or flatters; she is never unstable, changeable, or presumptuous. Charity "vaunteth not itself;" she is not puffed up with pride, but esteeming each one more worthy than herself, she shows due deference to all, "in honour preferring one another" (Rom. xii. 10). Charity "seeketh not her own;" she is wholly disinterested, and as her earthly happiness is centred in the welfare of others, she is far removed from all self-seeking. Charity "is not easily provoked;" she does not indulge in feelings of anger and irritation against others, but always preserves a spirit of good-will towards them, whatsoever cause of displeasure they may give her. Charity "thinketh no evil;" she never dwells upon it, but, especially if it be evil done to herself, she seeks to pass it over and to forgive and forget it. Charity "rejoiceth not in iniquity, but rejoiceth in the truth;" the evil life and the irregularities of her neighbour are to her no theme for light talk and amusement; but, on the contrary, her joy is to see him advance by the practice of virtue in the way of truth and righteousness. Charity "beareth all things;" and so great is her desire to persevere in the service of her neighbour, that no neglect, or sufferings, or temptations can ever discourage her, or shake her constancy. Charity "believeth all things;" she is always ready to credit the existence of good in others, and to think as favourably as possible of their motives. Charity "hopeth all things;" she never despairs of the conversion of the most hardened sinner, but continuing to believe the best of him, she trusts that he may yet find acceptance with GOD, and that all graces may be bestowed upon him. Charity "endureth all things;" never sinking under whatever burden may be laid upon her, but remaining ever unwearied and full of courage in the discharge of every duty. Let us ask ourselves whether such has been our frame of mind.

THIRD POINT.

O MY GOD, how happy should we be if, following the example of Thy Beloved Disciple, we had ever on our lips and in our hearts the precept of brotherly love. Give us this grace, we beseech Thee, O LORD; and grant that we may never forget the reply which, as S. Jerome relates, that great Apostle made to those of his followers who questioned him upon this subject; "This is the Commandment of the LORD Himself; and, if we fulfil it, it is all-sufficient."

Of the Love of our Neighbour.

SOME DEFECTS CONTRARY TO THIS VIRTUE.

FIRST POINT.

LET us adore the unapproachable Goodness and Lovingkindness of GOD as shown in the command which He gives us to love our neighbour, "Thou shalt love thy neighbour as thyself." The KING and LORD of all wills that we should love our brethren. He annexes the same reward to the fulfilment of this duty, the same penalty to the neglect thereof, as He promises in respect to the precept of the love of Himself: and so absolutely does He claim from all this virtue of brotherly love, that love shown to Himself alone, how fervent soever, cannot in His sight atone for its absence. Let us then reverently praise the GOD of Love, Who thus appears, if we may so speak, to forget His own claims upon us, in consideration of the debt which is due to our neighbour.

SECOND POINT.

LET us examine in what particulars we have been wanting in the love of our neighbour.

Firstly. Have we not been over-hasty in suspecting his motives and judging his conduct; and have we not been eager to communicate our unfavourable opinion of him to others?

Secondly. Have we not entertained thoughts of displeasure, anger, and hatred towards him, and have we not cherished these evil thoughts? Have we not, in consequence, avoided meeting him, or speaking to him, or shunned opportunities of serving him? Or, if we have spoken to him, have we not done so with bitter words and a cold, distant manner?

Thirdly. When we have any supposed cause of offence against him, do we not brood over our resentment, perhaps, even for several days? Have we not wished to be revenged upon him, or, at least, have we not experienced a feeling of satisfaction when he has failed in some undertaking, or has been turned into ridicule, or has been evil spoken of by others? Have we not ourselves calumniated him deliberately, and without cause—quieting our conscience with the idea that what we said could do him little harm, as it was perfectly true and generally known?

Lastly. Have we in all our dealings with our neighbour carefully followed the maxim of S. Jerome, " Never to give pain to others by any word, deed, or look whatsoever"?

THIRD POINT.

O MY GOD, since we cannot love Thee without also loving our neighbour, and since if we offend him we offend Thee likewise— " As ye have done it unto one of the least of these My brethren, ye have done it unto Me" (S. Matt. xxv. 40)—what cause for fear have those who give way to an unloving spirit. O LORD, I acknowledge that I have often sinned in this particular ; pardon me, I beseech Thee, and grant me Thy grace, that henceforth I may steadfastly follow the counsels of Thine Apostle, by crushing within me even the smallest seeds of hatred and bitterness against my neighbour : " Let all bitterness, and wrath, and anger, and clamour, and evil-speaking, be put away from you, with all malice" (Eph. iv. 31).

Of the Love of our Neighbour.

THE LOVE OF OUR ENEMIES.

FIRST POINT.

LET us adore our LORD JESUS CHRIST, Who, hanging upon the Cross, prayed for those who had condemned Him to death, " FATHER, forgive them ; for they know not what they do" (S. Luke xxiii. 34). He, our Divine Redeemer, in the pangs of death, covered with wounds from which His precious Blood flowed, and full of anguish, yet spent His last breath in praying for His persecutors. Oh, how Divine is this Example of forgiveness of enemies. Let us give humble thanks to our Blessed SAVIOUR for this His teaching.

SECOND POINT.

LET us examine whether we possess that charity to which the LORD JESUS exhorts us when He commands us to love our enemies. This charity requires us to love them, to speak favourably of them, to pray for them, to do them good. " I say unto you, Love your enemies, bless them that curse you, do good to them that hate you, and pray for them which despitefully use you, and persecute you" (S. Matt. v. 44). Have we faithfully fulfilled these precepts?

Firstly. Have we loved them—carefully rooting out from our hearts not merely all thoughts of revenge, but even the slightest trace of animosity towards them? Have we earnestly striven to cherish a feeling of real cordiality and good-will for them ; and have we sought opportunities of showing this feeling, instead of being satisfied with saying that we wish them no ill? Do we seek a reconciliation with them as soon as possible, in accordance with the counsel of the Apostle, "Let not the sun go down upon your wrath"? (Eph. iv. 26.) Have we made the first advances towards reconciliation with them, instead of delaying under the idea that they were more in fault than ourselves, and that therefore the first steps ought to be taken by them?

Secondly. Do we speak favourably of them—taking care not only to avoid exaggerating any cause of offence which they may have given us, but abstaining from the slightest allusion to it, and defending them when others speak against them; and in all points behaving in such a manner as to show that we are free from all ill-feeling towards them?

Thirdly. Have we prayed for them—remembering their needs before the Throne of GOD, and beseeching Him in their behalf with as much zeal and earnestness as we exert in putting up our own petitions?

Fourthly. Have we done good to them—assisting them with our counsel, our interest, and our purse, if necessary; anticipating their wants, whether corporal or spiritual, and serving them as readily and heartily as though they were our dearest-loved friends?

THIRD POINT.

O MY GOD, how can I offend those who hate me, when I remember that Thou lovest me, whom sin makes Thine enemy? How can I refrain from loving them, when I see that Thou seekest their love even whilst they transgress Thy Law? I now resolve by Thy grace, O LORD, to love all my enemies; and, whatever injuries they may inflict upon me, no shadow of resentment shall continue to darken my heart; that so I may with confidence repeat the Prayer which Thou Thyself didst teach unto us: "Forgive us our trespasses, as we forgive them that trespass against us."

Of the Christian's True Wisdom, and the Counsels thereof.

FIRST POINT.

LET us adore our Blessed SAVIOUR, filled with the SPIRIT of GOD, Which is the SPIRIT of all Wisdom and Knowledge. "The Spirit of the LORD shall rest upon Him, the Spirit of Wisdom and Understanding, the Spirit of Counsel and Might, the Spirit of Knowledge and of the Fear of the LORD" (Isa. xi. 2). Let us reverently contemplate the faithfulness with which our Divine Redeemer directed the whole of His earthly course by the Light of this Heavenly Wisdom, and let us give thanks to Him for having left us the same rule for our own guidance, both by His teaching, and by His life.

SECOND POINT.

LET us examine whether our lives are ruled in accordance with the maxims of true Christian Wisdom.

Firstly. He who governs himself by the maxims of this Heavenly Wisdom makes the Glory of GOD the leading principle of his life, and of his every action. "Seek ye first the Kingdom of GOD, and His righteousness" (S. Matt. vi. 33). He recognizes the infinite smallness of all the things of this world, and the absolute unimportance of every thing save the Love and Service of GOD. "Vanity of vanities; and all is vanity, but to love GOD and serve Him alone," says A Kempis. He considers that his first and greatest duty is to work out, with fear and trembling, his salvation; and he counts all gain as loss, should it endanger his soul. "What is a man profited, if he shall gain the whole world, and lose his own soul"? (S. Matt. xvi. 26.)

Secondly. In order to accomplish the great aim and end of his existence, he endeavours to tread exactly in the footsteps of his Divine Redeemer, asking no counsel of human reason, but walking by the light of faith alone. If the choice of circumstances be offered him, and if all appear to be equally in conformity with the Will of GOD, he will, after the example of the Great Master, prefer poverty to riches, a lowly station to exalted rank, a life of suffering to a life of worldly pleasure. " Looking unto JESUS . . . . . . Who for the joy that was set before Him endured the Cross, despising the shame" (Heb. xii. 2). Knowing that all perfection is comprised in fulfilling the Will of GOD, and in obeying Him without reserve, he rejoices to lead a life of perfect submission, and undertakes from preference whatever tasks afford most opportunities of practising obedience.

Thirdly. In order faithfully to carry out, as far as in him lies, the great work of his salvation, he watches unceasingly, remembering the words of our Blessed LORD in the Gospel, " Watch therefore, for ye know neither the day nor the hour wherein the SON of Man cometh" (S. Matt. xxv. 13). He watches, lest he should miss any opportunity of putting in practice the precepts which he has chosen for his guidance : he watches, whether the task allotted to him be great or small, in order that he may be found faithful in all things : he watches, fearing lest he should be assailed and overcome by his ghostly enemy. Let us examine whether our lives have been ruled by these maxims of Christian Wisdom.

THIRD POINT.

ALMIGHTY GOD, what cause for shame have we, Thy Children, when we reflect how far wiser are the children of this World as regards their temporal concerns, than we are in pursuing the all-important work of our salvation. Thou knowest, O LORD, how great are the dangers to which we are exposed, and how powerful is the Enemy of our souls. Hear us then, we beseech Thee, in the words of the Church's Advent supplication, " O Wisdom, Which camest forth out of the Mouth of the Most High, and reachest from one end to the other, mightily and sweetly ordering all things ; Come and teach us the way of prudence."

Of Humility.

THE ESTEEM AND LOVE WE SHOULD HAVE FOR THIS VIRTUE.

FIRST POINT.

LET us adore our LORD JESUS CHRIST, Whose sacred Heart was filled with love for the virtue of humility, of which He has deigned to give us so many beautiful examples. He was born in poverty, He lived in obscurity, He died a death accounted shameful; and He has promised His grace to the humble, who are ever well-pleasing to Him. In truth, it may be said that He came on earth to teach us humility: "Learn of Me; for I am meek and lowly in heart" (S. Matt. xi. 29).

SECOND POINT.

LET us ask ourselves whether we have duly loved and honoured the virtue of humility.

Have we considered it, as did the Saints of GOD, as being the root and foundation of all other virtues, as the true throne of grace, and the very crown of the elect?

Do we take pleasure in meditating upon this virtue?

Do we sincerely desire to acquire it, and do we earnestly beg of GOD that it may be granted to us?

Have we allowed ourselves to be swayed by the opinion of the world, which despises humility, and looks upon it as a virtue only fitted for the cloister, considering those who practise it as being devoid of courage and energy, and therefore utterly unsuited for public life?

Instead of thinking thus, do we reverence those who make

choice of a hidden life, and who, desiring to share in this world the humiliations of our Divine Redeemer, partake most abundantly of His graces here, and share most largely in the glory of His Saints hereafter [1]?

Do we from love of humility seek rather to associate with those who are lowliest and of least esteem in the eyes of the world, than with those who are more conspicuous by position or by talent?

Do we try to inspire others with a love of humility, and do we strive to point out to them its beauty, and, as far as we can, to make it attractive to them?

"All of you be subject one to another, and be clothed with humility" (1 S. Pet. v. 5).

THIRD POINT.

O LORD, I know that although Thou art Most High, yet Thou hast "respect unto the lowly" (Ps. cxxxviii. 6), and it was because this virtue of humility was most pleasing to Thee, that Thou didst choose the Blessed Virgin to be the Mother of our Emmanuel. "He hath regarded the low estate of His Handmaiden" (S. Luke i. 48). By this Thou hast shown the greatness of Thy favour to the humble. Implant in me, then, I beseech Thee, O my GOD, the grace of humility, and grant that from henceforth I may look upon all humiliations as privileges, given by Thee, to be received with joy, and used to the benefit of my soul and to the glory of Thy holy Name.

[1] "Still to the lowly soul
He doth Himself impart;
And for His cradle and His Throne
Chooseth the pure in heart."
Christian Year.

Of Humility.

SELF-KNOWLEDGE IS THE CHIEF FOUNDATION OF THIS VIRTUE.

FIRST POINT.

LET us adore our LORD JESUS CHRIST, Who, although, as GOD, He is co-equal with His FATHER, yet, as Man, shows us by His own Example how we should prostrate ourselves before the Divine Majesty, acknowledging our nothingness in His Presence. "Mine age is as nothing before Thee" (Ps. xxxix. 5). Nothing is more calculated to fill us with awe and reverence than the spectacle of the World's Redeemer thus proclaiming the subjection of His Human Nature.

SECOND POINT.

LET us examine whether we possess any real self-knowledge, and whether we continually bear in mind what we are.

Do we remember that we spring from nothing; that we have no power over these frail lives of ours, which proceed from nothing; and that, were we not upheld by the mighty Hand of GOD, we should return again to nothing?

Are we fully persuaded that we can call nothing our own; that we are nothing; and that we can do nothing of ourselves; no, not even conceive a single good thought? "Not that we are sufficient of ourselves to think any thing as of ourselves; but our sufficiency is of GOD" (2 Cor. iii. 5).

Do we remember that having offended GOD, sin has reduced us to less than nothing, because it adds to our nothingness the guilt of treason against the Divine Majesty? For, as S. Ambrose says, "Sin is simply an atom in armed rebellion against GOD."

Lastly, do we acknowledge that we are so corrupt and so prone to evil, that even such of our actions as seem to be good are full of imperfections; and that, however fair our lives may appear in outward show, our shortcomings are indeed great and manifold? "Thou sayest, I am rich, and increased with goods, and have need of nothing; and knowest not that thou art wretched, and miserable, and poor, and blind, and naked" (Rev. iii. 17).

THIRD POINT.

O MY GOD, since Thy Saints have declared that there can be no true humility save that which is founded on self-knowledge, fulfil in me, I pray Thee, the petition of S. Augustine: "Grant me, O LORD, Thy grace, that I may know what Thou art, and what I am."

Of Humility.

THE FIRST DEGREE OF THIS VIRTUE IS TO ESTEEM OURSELVES LOWLY.

FIRST POINT.

LET us continue to adore in our Blessed SAVIOUR His lowly estimation of Himself as Man, speaking thus of Himself by the mouth of His Prophet : " I am a worm, and no man ; a reproach of men, and despised of the people" (Ps. xxii. 6). Let us with reverence meditate upon this wonderful Humility of our dear LORD, and let us offer up to Him our grateful and loving praises.

SECOND POINT.

HAVE we kept in constant remembrance our own nothingness and sinfulness, so as to maintain a genuinely humble opinion of ourselves?

Even should GOD be pleased to confer any graces upon us, do we earnestly combat all feelings of self-elation, remembering the example given us by the Blessed Virgin, who was never more fully penetrated with the conviction of her own "low estate" in the sight of GOD, than at the moment when she was raised by Him above all creatures?

"Then," says S. Ambrose, "she whom GOD chose to be His Mother, acknowledged herself to be His Handmaiden." Do we not quickly lose this consciousness of our nothingness when we are flattered and applauded by the world ; and do we not suffer ourselves to be dazzled and intoxicated by praise, instead of humbling ourselves and saying, as did S. Ignatius, "Those who praise me, scourge me[1]"?

When others appear to love us and esteem us, do we not feel shame for ourselves and compassion for their blindness—knowing that if they could see us as we really are, they would quickly change their opinion of us?

Does the conviction of our own weakness have the salutary effect of keeping us continually on the watch—as being well aware that there are no temptations, how small soever, which are not capable of becoming the cause of our eternal ruin?

When we find ourselves cast down and discouraged by the contemplation of our sinfulness, are we not too prone to rouse ourselves by banishing these thoughts as quickly as possible, and by dwelling upon such points in our character as we imagine to be deserving of admiration?

Lastly, with whatever talents it may have pleased our Master to endow us, are we so thoroughly grounded in humility as to remember constantly that these gifts are but lent to us as a trust to be accounted for, and that since they are not ours, they can in no sense be a legitimate cause for pride or vainglory?

THIRD POINT.

O MY GOD, I do indeed find in myself sufficient grounds for humiliation : but though my sins humble me, Thy mercies alone can give me the grace of humility. Grant me, then, this grace, O LORD, that so, casting aside all vain and false ideas of my own merit, I may be henceforth fully impressed with my own unworthiness : and thus, as says the author of the *Imitation*, "all self-estimation, how small soever, will be sunk in the depths of my own nothingness, and there be lost for ever."

[1] "Pray we our LORD one pang to send
Of deep remorseful fear,
For every smile of partial friend;
Praise be our penance here."
Lyra Innocentium.

Of Humility.

THE SECOND DEGREE OF THIS VIRTUE MAKES US REJOICE WHEN WE ARE HUMBLED.

FIRST POINT.

LET us adore our LORD JESUS CHRIST filling the heart of S. Paul to so great a degree with His Spirit of Humility as that the Apostle suffered humiliations not only patiently but joyfully, saying, "Most gladly therefore will I rather glory in my infirmities" (2 Cor. xii. 9). He often speaks of these infirmities in his Epistles, acknowledging that, although it had pleased GOD to grant him many and singular graces, yet of himself he found nothing wherein to glory save in his infirmities. "Of myself I will not glory, but in mine infirmities" (2 Cor. xii. 5). Let us recognize the truth of this feeling, and let us bless the LORD JESUS Who inspired it, from Whom all good thoughts come.

SECOND POINT.

HAS our lowly esteem of ourselves been accompanied by patience, and have we accustomed ourselves to consider calmly, without repining, whatever circumstances are most calculated to humiliate us?

Are we not apt, from a false spirit of humility, to give way to moodiness and melancholy, withdrawing ourselves from all social intercourse, under the impression that, to be humble, we ought to live in solitude and shun our fellow-creatures?

When we are treated with contempt by others, do we look upon this as a favour sent from GOD for which we can never be sufficiently grateful; and do we from our hearts repeat the words of the Psalmist, who, after recording the reproaches and derision wherewith he had been assailed, says with sincere humility, "It is good for me that I have been afflicted?" (Ps. cxix. 71.)

Are we so truly inclined to think humbly of ourselves as to be ready to accept any obscure employment in preference to a more conspicuous post?

Lastly, have we rejoiced in the conviction of our own nothingness—acknowledging that of ourselves we are utterly powerless, and that we are so wholly dependent upon GOD, that we cannot exist for one moment, or take one single step without Him? "Without Me ye can do nothing" (S. John xv. 5).

THIRD POINT.

O MY GOD, since true humility fills us with that conviction of our own nothingness, and that desire to remain as nothing and to suffer humiliations for Thy sake wherein alone true joy can be found[1]; give me, I pray Thee, a share in that grace which Thou didst bestow upon the kingly Prophet, who rejoiced to abase himself in his own eyes and in the sight of others for the love of Thee. "I will be yet more vile than thus, and will be base in mine own sight" (2 Sam. vi. 22).

---

[1] "He can endless glory weave
From what men reckon shame."
F. W. FABER.

Of Pride.

FIRST POINT.

LET us adore the infinite Justice of GOD as displayed in the dread penalty inflicted upon the rebel Angels, whose sin of pride brought upon them this fearful retribution. No sooner had they in their mad presumption conceived the thought of raising themselves to an equality with the Divine Majesty, than they were cast down from the highest Heaven to the lowest depths of the abyss. Let us reflect with awe upon this their punishment. "If these things were done to the Angels," says S. Bernard, "what shall be done to me, who am but dust and ashes?"

SECOND POINT.

PRIDE is an inordinate love and admiration of ourselves, and of the good qualities which we suppose ourselves to possess. Many are guilty of this sin in divers ways.

Firstly. Those whose great desire it is to be esteemed by others.

Secondly. Those who from this self-glorifying spirit affect, like the Pharisees, to be more devout and virtuous than they really are.

Thirdly. Those who are ever talking of themselves, and who delight in hearing their own praises.

Fourthly. Those who think constantly of honours, dignities, and high offices: who imagine that they deserve greatness, and who continually seek to achieve it.

Fifthly. Those who have so high an opinion of their own abilities that they engage without hesitation in the most difficult undertakings, which they are altogether incapable of conducting to the end.

Sixthly. Those who from an excess of confidence in their own powers of intellect despise all counsel, even when given by their spiritual Superiors.

Lastly. Those who, wishing at all costs to raise themselves, depreciate whatever is done by others : acting upon the maxim that to raise oneself one must hold every body else in contempt.

THIRD POINT.

O ALL-JUST and Merciful LORD, how important is the lesson to be drawn from the fall of the rebel Angels. Hereby we learn that this sin of pride has power to corrupt the purest and to conquer the strongest, and that it can even find an entrance into the holiest places. Grant, we pray Thee, that we may lay these thoughts to heart, and that thus, through Thy grace, to use S. Bernard's words, "The Angels' fall may help to raise us from the abyss of our sins."

Of Vanity.

FIRST POINT.

LET us adore our LORD JESUS CHRIST rebuking the Scribes and Pharisees for their vaingloriousness, which led them to seek in all their actions the esteem and applause of mankind. "When thou doest thine alms, do not sound a trumpet before thee, as the hypocrites do in the synagogues and in the streets, that they may have glory of men" (S. Matt. vi. 2). He reproves them sternly, and commands His Disciples and His people to beware of acting in like manner under pain of losing the promised reward in the Heavenly Kingdom; "otherwise ye have no reward of your FATHER Which is in Heaven" (S. Matt. vi. 1). Let us meditate reverently upon His detestation of all vaingloriousness, and let us return thanks to Him for manifesting to us thus plainly His desire that we should avoid the snares of this sin.

SECOND POINT.

VANITY excites in us an inordinate passion for receiving the admiration and applause of our fellow-creatures. Let us examine whether we are not subject to this sin.

Do we not eagerly desire to fill the highest and most important posts—disdaining such as appear obscure and humble?

If we are in Holy Orders, are we not more anxious to preach than to catechize—or to be appointed to the cure of a town parish with an educated population, rather than to be placed in a remote district amongst rude and uncultivated people?

Is it not from vanity that we devote ourselves to study, and that we strive hard to excel in some branch of learning or science?

Does not vanity cause us to affect singularity in our opinions, our tastes, and our habits, and to adopt readily every novel theory, particularly as regards sacred things?

Has not this vainglorious spirit led us to be constant in attendance at Divine Service, though without having any real fervour in our prayers; to be diligent in frequenting the holy Sacraments, without making any true resolutions of amendment; and, in short, to go through our religious duties as a mere matter of routine, in order to maintain a reputation for respectability?

When we acknowledge ourselves to be miserable sinners, helpless and ignorant, and unfit to guide our own course through life, do we not cherish a secret hope that we shall be praised for our humility in making this avowal, instead of desiring in all sincerity to be known for what we really are?

Do we not delight in hearing our own praises, even though we know them to be undeserved—caring nothing for what we are in the sight of GOD, but only for what the world judges us to be?

Lastly, instead of using the talents which GOD has given us to promote His glory, do we not think chiefly or wholly of advancing ourselves by their means, thus, like the Pharisees, loving "the praise of men more than the praise of GOD"? (S. John xii. 43.)

THIRD POINT.

O MY GOD, how blind are those who seek worldly glory, which is but smoke and vapour, quickly vanishing away, yet taxing the utmost powers of those who strive to attain it. Deliver me, O LORD, I beseech Thee, from so common and so fatal an error. Open Thou mine eyes, that I may see where alone my love and service should be given, and that I may no longer spend myself on so unworthy an object as the fleeting glory of this world, which one of Thy servants has well compared to "a buzzing insect, feeding on what is vile and sordid, and leaving a sharp sting in him who attempts to seize upon it."

Of Presumption and Self-Confidence.

FIRST POINT.

LET us adore the infinite Justice of ALMIGHTY GOD, which permitted S. Peter to fall into the great sin of denying his Master, in rebuke of his over-great self-confidence. S. Peter had vowed to remain faithful to his LORD, even though all should forsake Him; yet he fell, because he trusted in his own strength. And his sin should make all presumptuous souls tremble; for, as S. Bernard says, "When even S. Peter fell, who can dare to be sure of himself?" Let us return thanks to GOD for the warning here afforded us, and let us ask His grace to enable us to profit by it.

SECOND POINT.

THE presumptuous man is full of confidence in his own powers, and has an absurdly exaggerated opinion of his own merits. He does not believe that there is a single weak point in his character which should cause him to distrust himself. He imagines himself to be capable of any undertaking, and of succeeding in every thing. He thinks himself more enlightened than the rest of mankind, and therefore he will listen to no advice even in spiritual matters. It is useless to repeat to him that the Saints of GOD have constantly insisted upon the necessity of having a Director; for he does not for one moment admit that he can possibly require one. Should it please GOD to bestow upon him any graces or spiritual favours, he imagines himself to be specially distinguished on account of his own merits, and considers himself to be entitled even to farther proofs of the Divine Bounty. So long as he contrives to avoid mortal sin, and does not fall into very serious irregularities, his mind is in a frame of perpetual self-complacency. Instead of being covered with confusion when he thinks of his many failings which are still unconquered, he is as perfectly at ease as though he had received a positive assurance of salvation. If he is forced to admit that some of his neighbours are gifted with talents which he does not possess, he still flatters himself that in other respects he far excels them: and he never supposes that his deficiencies can be caused by any fault of his own. He is ever desirous of receiving marks of deference from those about him. Lastly, from being exclusively occupied with himself, he becomes as it were a self-worshipper, holding all others as immeasurably beneath him, and thinking no opinion worth listening to but his own. Let us examine whether our presumption and self-confidence may not have led us into some of these errors.

THIRD POINT.

O MY GOD, Thine Apostle has told us that Thou dost resist the proud, whilst to the humble Thou dost give grace (S. James iv. 6). Give us then, we beseech Thee, that grace which may enable us to keep the resolution which we now firmly make— never from henceforth to rely upon our own strength, but to put our trust in Thee alone.

Of Patience.

PATIENCE AS A VIRTUE.

FIRST POINT.

LET us adore our LORD JESUS CHRIST, Who upon Mount Calvary offered to us the most perfect Example of Patience—the "pattern which was" shown us "in the Mount" (Exod. xxv. 40). He there suffered the most cruel pangs, yet did His Patience, as S. Augustine says, surpass the measure of His sufferings, that He might thereby teach us patience. How can we thank and praise our Loving SAVIOUR as we ought when we contemplate Him thus suffering for our instruction?

SECOND POINT.

HE who is truly patient suffers silently, and in perfect calmness, whatever afflictions and trials may be appointed for him. He knows so well the source wherein he can quench all sorrow, that howsoever his mind may be stirred by emotion, his heart remains tranquil and unruffled, and neither in look, voice, nor manner does he betray sullenness, impatience, or querulousness. He preserves this inward peace under all circumstances, however trying, whether his afflictions be external or internal, bodily or spiritual. "There shall no evil happen to the just" (Prov. xii. 21). He does not merely accept his sufferings without a murmur—for this indeed is but the lowest step on the ladder of Patience—but he strives to endure them joyfully in the Spirit of Divine Love, which is the highest degree of this virtue. However great his trials may be, he is firmly resolved to do nothing displeasing to GOD, even if by so doing he might escape them. When human nature is too strong for him, obliging grief to have its course, he indulges in no excess of sorrow, but bows humbly to the Divine Will. He, nevertheless, does not flatter himself with the hope of having attained the grace of patience, for he knows how common is self-deception upon this point, and that what appears to be patience may be the effect of insensibility, or of some contending feeling so overmastering as to stifle grief. Lastly, he feels a great love and esteem for the virtue of patience, as being the first-fruits of charity, since S. Paul tells us that "charity suffereth long" (1 Cor. xiii. 4); and also as being the crown of all virtues, as we are assured by S. James. "Let patience have her perfect work, that ye may be perfect and entire, wanting nothing" (S. James i. 4). Let us try by these tests whether we are truly patient.

THIRD POINT.

O MY GOD, how lovely does the virtue of patience appear to us when we remember that Thy Saints have assured us that they who possess it obey Thee, and become like unto CHRIST. Open Thou yet more our eyes, we pray Thee, to behold the beauty of this great virtue, and grant that we Thy Children may ever strive to acquire and to practise that which, as our Master, Thou dost command, and of which Thou, as our FATHER, dost Thyself give us the Example; for, says S. Cyprian, "As servants, it is our duty to obey; as sons, it behoves us not to degenerate."

Of Patience.

PATIENCE UNDER SPECIAL TRIALS.

FIRST POINT.

LET us adore the Patience of our LORD JESUS CHRIST, pre-figured in the wonderful patience of the Patriarch Job, who endured, with the most perfect submission to the Divine Will, the loss of children, goods, and wealth, saying only, " The LORD gave, and the LORD hath taken away ; blessed be the Name of the LORD" (Job i. 21). And even so, though in an infinitely more perfect manner, did our Blessed SAVIOUR suffer His Agony in the garden, " Not My Will, but Thine, be done" (S. Luke xxii. 42). Oh, how beautiful is this Patience—how worthy of our reverent adoration.

SECOND POINT.

LET us examine whether we have shown patience under all trials which we may have been called upon to undergo.

If we are born poor, and if it is the will of GOD that we should continue to live in a state of poverty, do we not murmur against His decrees and give way to fretfulness and discontent?

If we are born to the possession of riches, or if we have attained them by our own exertions, and are deprived of them by any unforeseen accident, do we bear our losses cheerfully as did the early Christians, of whom S. Paul tells us that they " took joyfully the spoiling of" their " goods, knowing " in themselves that they had " in heaven a better and an enduring substance"? (Heb. x. 34.)

If, under GOD'S Providence, others are the cause of our having to endure hardships, do we not cherish a feeling of anger and bitterness against them?

Are we not impatient and undisciplined in spirit if we have to bear any insult or mortification, or if we are calumniated in any way?

Do we not give way to immoderate grief when death deprives us of any of our friends or relatives, instead of seeking consolation in prayer for them, and in resignation to the will of an All-wise and All-merciful GOD [1]?

Are we not restless and depressed under spiritual sufferings—such as dryness and coldness in prayer, weariness, dread of GOD'S anger, and other trials which He is pleased to permit from time to time in order to strengthen our faith; instead of having recourse to prayer and works of charity, to a careful avoidance of the smallest sin, and to a perfect and entire trust in GOD?

Lastly, whatever afflictions and troubles may overtake us, do we submit ourselves calmly and in peace, like the Kingly Prophet, who in his deepest anguish kept his heart stayed upon the LORD, and thought only of obeying His adorable Will: "Trouble and anguish have taken hold on me: yet Thy commandments are my delights"? (Ps. cxix. 143.)

THIRD POINT.

HOW happy are those, O my GOD, who have both understood and put in practice the blessed mystery of Martyrdom, in the peace of Thy Church. "There are Martyrs also even in the

---

[1] "... Since our souls will shrink
  At the touch of natural grief,
  When our earthly loved ones sink,
  Lend us, LORD, Thy sure relief:
  Patient hearts, their pain to see,
  And Thy grace, to follow Thee!"
  Christian Year.—S. John's Day.

Patience under Special Trials.

peace of Thy Church," says S. Augustine : these are they whose privilege it is to suffer Martyrdom in will by their patience under afflictions [2]. It is from Thee, O JESUS, that we look for the gift of this virtue—for, as one of Thy servants has said, " Thou hast taught it to us by Thy Example, and Thou dost Thyself vouchsafe to be its exceeding great Reward."

[2] "Nor deem, who to that bliss aspire,
Must win their way through blood and fire.
* * * *
Meek souls there are, who little dream
Their daily strife an angel's theme,
Or that the rod they take so calm
Shall prove in heaven a martyr's palm."
Christian Year.—Wednesday before Easter.

Of Patience.

FAULTS TO BE AVOIDED IN TIME OF SICKNESS.

FIRST POINT.

LET us adore our Blessed LORD giving Himself up, without one word of remonstrance or complaint, to be bound, and scourged, and nailed to the Cross. "He is brought as a lamb to the slaughter, and as a sheep before her shearers is dumb, so He openeth not His mouth" (Isa. liii. 7). Here we find a most perfect rule to be followed by us when sickness confines us to our bed or our chamber.

SECOND POINT.

THE faults most usually committed by sick persons who do not keep a very careful watch over themselves, are as follows :—

Firstly. Thinking chiefly of their illness, talking about it perpetually, and not caring for any other subject of conversation.

Secondly. Giving way to impatience when their requests are not immediately complied with, or if they are kept waiting for any thing.

Thirdly. Restlessness and excitability, irritation and fretfulness of manner towards those who attend upon them, and discontent with whatever is done for them.

Fourthly. Moroseness and a sullen disinclination to speak.

Fifthly. Excessive dread of pain, and an over-great eagerness to find relief and to be restored to health.

Sixthly. Neglect of all rules of self-discipline.

Faults to be avoided in Time of Sickness.

Let us examine whether we have not been guilty of these faults.

THIRD POINT.

O MY GOD, one of Thy holy servants has well said that "few persons become better by sickness," because there are few who do not, in time of sickness, give way to impatience, to querulousness, to moroseness, and to many similar faults. It is these faults, O LORD, which it must be my care henceforth to avoid. Grant me, therefore, I pray Thee, some share in the grace which Thou didst bestow upon Thine Apostle, enabling him to say, "My strength is made perfect in weakness . . . . . Therefore I take pleasure in infirmities . . . . . for when I am weak, then am I strong" (2 Cor. xii. 9, 10).

Of Patience.

THE LESSONS TAUGHT US BY SICKNESS.

FIRST POINT.

LET us adore our LORD JESUS CHRIST hanging upon the Cross, bearing "our griefs" and carrying "our sorrows" (Isa. liii. 4), and showing us by His Example how many lessons are to be derived from the trials which are appointed for us. Let us contemplate Him upon this bed of pain; let us meditate upon His perfect resignation, His unshrinking courage, His wonderful patience amidst the most cruel tortures. What can be more worthy of our loving and reverent adoration?

SECOND POINT.

LET us now see how we have behaved in time of sickness, and what lessons we have learnt therefrom.

Have we looked upon bodily sickness with the eye of faith, as being a remedy for the diseases of the soul, as a portion of our LORD'S Cross, and as a precious gift from the Hand of our Loving FATHER?

Looking upon it in this light, do we accept it joyfully, or at all events, submissively?

Has not our excessive solicitude about the human means employed for our relief caused us to neglect our spiritual medicines—the Sacraments of the Church of GOD—as though the health of the body was more important than the health of the soul?

Have we borne our sickness in a spirit of contrition, uniting our sufferings to those of our Blessed SAVIOUR, and offering them to Him?

Do we resign ourselves at such times wholly to the Will of GOD, in Whose Hands are the issues of life and death ; remaining for our own part in a state of entire indifference, like S. Martin, of whom we read that "he feared not death, neither did he refuse to live"?

Do we submit instantly, and without demur, to whatever remedies are proposed?

If the bitterness of the medicines prescribed for us cause repugnance, do we, when taking them, try to think of the gall and vinegar which our LORD tasted upon the Cross, and do we beg Him to give us a share in His Cup?

Do we ask the Blessing of GOD upon the remedies employed for our cure ; and if it is not His pleasure that they should be successful, do we accept the decree without murmuring?

When our illness prevents us from offering up our accustomed prayers, do we endeavour to supply their place by frequent ejaculations and elevations of the heart towards GOD?

And is it our constant aim to practise all those virtues compatible with a state of sickness—such as ready obedience to the orders of our physicians, submission to our spiritual superiors, thankfulness to those who wait upon us, and gentleness to all about us—that so we may profit by those lessons which sickness is intended to teach us?

THIRD POINT.

O MY GOD, it is related of one of Thy Saints, that, having been long unvisited by sickness, he wept, thinking that he was forsaken by Thee, and that Thou didst refuse him a share in Thy Cross. This was a proof that he fully understood how precious a means of grace bodily suffering may become. Give me, I beseech Thee, some portion of his spirit; that thus, although I may not be able, like him, to desire sufferings, I may yet patiently endure all which Thou dost send me : and may Thy grace make them profitable to me.

Of Recovery from Sickness.

FIRST POINT.

LET us adore the LORD our GOD, "Who healeth all" our "diseases" (Ps. ciii. 3). The chief snare into which we are liable to fall when recovering from sickness is, that being much occupied with the restoration of our bodily health, we are in danger of neglecting our spiritual concerns. Only by great faithfulness to the grace which we have received can this snare be avoided: but this gift of faithfulness is never refused by our Blessed LORD to those who ask it with a firm confidence in Him. "Ask, and it shall be given you" (S. Matt. vii. 7). Let us give thanks for this as for all other proofs of His great Goodness to us.

SECOND POINT.

WHEN we are recovering from illness, do we remember that, in a spiritual sense, we can hardly be in a more critical state, since at such times we are, in a manner, obliged to think a great deal about the re-establishment of our health; and therefore we are in great danger of falling into self-indulgent habits?

Have we yielded to the temptation of gluttony; looking forward with pleasure to our meals, and imagining that, as our strength needed recruiting, we might lawfully gratify our palate to the full extent?

Have we given way to sloth and indolence, under the idea that, not being able to exert ourselves as much as usual, we might be dispensed from all occupations, even the least fatiguing?

Have we not put off from day to day the resumption of our ordinary employments, instead of returning to them gradually,

Of Recovery from Sickness.

and endeavouring each day to do more and more according to our increased strength?

Have we not also been unwilling to resume our accustomed devotions—fancying that the mental exertion required was too great for us in our weakened condition?

Have we not shrunk from conversing with devout persons on religious subjects—looking upon such topics as too serious and depressing?

Have we not imagined that it was necessary for us to divert our minds, and to amuse ourselves as much as possible; and that consequently we were at liberty to choose whatever recreations we preferred; to pass our time in idle and unprofitable conversation; and, in short, to emancipate ourselves completely from all rules and restraints?

And, lastly, have we not, on these accounts, found this state of recovery to be so agreeable as to be desirous of prolonging it as much as possible?

THIRD POINT.

O MY GOD, Thou knowest how full of pitfalls is the road leading from sickness on to health, and how difficult it is to pass over it unscathed. Preserve us, O LORD, we beseech Thee, from these dangers; and let us not be of the number of those whose souls become more feeble as their bodies regain strength, and by whom the health which Thou hast restored to them is abused, as though it had been given to them but for their own pleasure, and not for Thy honour and glory.

Of Sloth.

FIRST POINT.

LET us adore our LORD JESUS CHRIST, Who, in order to implant in us a great abhorrence of sloth, gives us in His Gospel three very remarkable examples of the penalties attached to this vice. He condemns the unprofitable servant, in the parable of the talents, to be cast into the outer darkness (S. Matt. xxv. 30). He orders all unfruitful trees to be hewn down and cast into the fire (S. Matt. iii. 10). And, by the mouth of His Apostle, He declares that the earth which beareth only thorns and briars is rejected (Heb. vi. 8). Under these figures we behold the sentence recorded against the slothful. Let us earnestly strive to shake off the fetters of this sin.

SECOND POINT.

LET us ask ourselves whether we really hate sloth as much as we ought to hate it.

Do we fly from "idleness" as being a vice which, the Son of Sirach tells us, "teacheth much evil" (Ecclus. xxxiii. 27)—for, in point of fact, sloth is usually either directly or indirectly the cause of the most heinous sins; and Ezekiel says, "This was the iniquity of Sodom, pride, fulness of bread, and abundance of idleness"? (Ezek. xvi. 49.) And do we remember that many eminent servants of GOD, after having escaped all other rocks and shoals, have been wrecked upon this one; and that David, Solomon, and Samson, who had led godly lives whilst they laboured, fell into sin through sloth?

Have we considered that a state of sloth is beyond all others subject to temptation; and that, as many of the Fathers of the Desert have observed, whilst only one evil spirit assails the busy man, hundreds make war upon the slothful?

And do we reflect that even when sloth does not give rise to such dreadful evils, it is nevertheless the cause of innumerable lesser sins—of wandering thoughts, of unfulfilled resolves, of idle talk and slander, of restless curiosity—making us, in a word, become like those Thessalonians of whom S. Paul thus speaks: "There are some which walk among you disorderly, working not at all, but are busybodies"? (2 Thess. iii. 11.)

Instead of trying to cherish a hatred of sloth in our minds, do we not accustom ourselves rather to look upon idleness in the light of an advantage, and even to envy those who are not obliged to work?

Have we not longed to be able ourselves to live in a state of idleness? And have we not, in order to enjoy a short interval of indolence, either neglected to fulfil some of our most important duties, or transferred them to another person?

Lastly, have we remembered that sloth is a sin which, as one of the servants of GOD expresses himself, weakens and numbs the soul, which stifles virtue and fosters vice, and which, if not rooted out in time, may become the cause of our eternal condemnation?

THIRD POINT.

O MY GOD, both in Thy Word and in the writings of Thy Saints, no point is more strongly insisted upon than that of the great dread and hatred of sloth which we should entertain; yet, in practice, how few do we find who have not some taint of this sin —how few who earnestly strive to avoid it. Do Thou, O LORD, inspire us with the love of work, and make us, we beseech Thee, feel how culpable we are if we, who have sinned, desire to shun a task which Thou didst allot to our first parents whilst yet they were in the state of innocence: "The LORD GOD took the man, and put him into the garden of Eden to dress it and to keep it" (Gen. ii. 15).

Of Temptations

HOW WE SHOULD BEAR OURSELVES WHEN ASSAILED BY TEMPTATIONS.

FIRST POINT.

LET us adore the wonderful goodness of our LORD JESUS CHRIST, Who for our sakes suffered Himself, All-Holy as He was, to be tempted by the Spirit of evil. "The Spirit driveth Him into the wilderness. And He was there in the wilderness forty days, tempted of Satan" (S. Mark i. 12, 13). Let us meditate upon this great humiliation—the greatest which could be endured by Him Who is the LORD and Maker of all things—which He was pleased to undergo for our example, in order that He might win for us the grace of resisting that evil Spirit and of overcoming all his temptations. "CHRIST therefore was tempted," says S. Augustine, "lest the Christian should be vanquished by the Tempter."

SECOND POINT.

THOSE who bear themselves rightly under temptations are not greatly troubled or dismayed when they find themselves assailed thereby, knowing that this life is an unceasing warfare, wherein men wrestle "not against flesh and blood, but against principalities, against powers, against the rulers of the darkness of this world" (Eph. vi. 12). Thus, since they expect temptation, and are ever ready to meet it, remembering the counsel of the Son of Sirach, "My son, if thou come to serve the LORD, prepare thy soul for temptation" (Ecclus. ii. 1), they still preserve a perfect peace of mind even when they are most sharply assaulted.

If they feel at times weary and cast down, they rouse themselves by the reflection that GOD wills faith to be put to the test and refined, as it were, in the furnace of temptation; and that He Himself watches their combat, and—as S. Augustine says in his Commentary on the Thirty-third Psalm—"sustains them when they falter, and crowns them when they have conquered." They do not give the temptation time to acquire any hold upon their minds, but do battle with it at once, and never relax till they have gained a complete victory. They humble themselves in the time of temptation, looking upon what they suffer as being but the just retribution of their sins: therefore, instead of murmuring, they submit with meekness, and implore the Divine grace to enable them to make a good use of this trial. They know that one of the most usual devices of the Evil One when he wishes to lead the servants of GOD into great sins is to begin with very trivial temptations which appear to be of no moment; and for this reason they are equally upon their guard against all, fighting as valiantly with the least as with the greatest; for they know that, as S. Jerome saith, "GOD watches with an equal eye over the least, as over the most important things." Lastly, they neglect none of those weapons wherewith the Saints of GOD have armed themselves against temptation—such as, distrust of themselves, confidence in Almighty GOD, union of heart with our Blessed SAVIOUR, and, above all things, constant watchfulness and prayer, in obedience to the Divine command, "Watch and pray, that ye enter not into temptation" (S. Matt. xxvi. 41).

THIRD POINT.

MOST Gracious GOD, Who dost permit that our faith should be tried by the multitude of evil spirits who seek our ruin, strengthen us, we beseech Thee, in our resolve to use every effort to resist and to overcome them. This do we look for, trusting in Thine infinite Goodness, O All-merciful FATHER, Who hast promised to be near us in all our temptations, and Whose might will give us the victory. "I will be with him in trouble: I will deliver him, and honour him" (Ps. xci. 15).

Of Temptations.

SPECIAL TEMPTATION

FIRST POINT.

LET us contemplate our LORD JESUS CHRIST, assailed at all points by the evil Spirit, and this in the most appalling manner. He is set upon a pinnacle of the Temple. He is carried up into an exceeding high mountain. Temptations of all kinds are held out to Him—temptations of pride, of ambition, of idolatry. Thus was He "in all points tempted like as we are, yet without sin" (Heb. iv. 15). Let us give thanks to our Blessed SAVIOUR, Who, for our example, was pleased to undergo the assaults of the enemy of mankind, and to put him to flight that we also might learn how to withstand him.

SECOND POINT.

LET us examine whether we have faithfully made use of all those means which have been prescribed to us by the Saints of GOD for overcoming our besetting temptations.

In temptations against faith, do we at once renounce all idea of setting ourselves to combat the doubts suggested by the evil Spirit, and do we at once take refuge in prayer; making acts of our belief in the doctrines of CHRIST and of His Church, and remembering that, since our GOD is a GOD of all Power and all Truth, we are bound to believe all which He commands us to believe, how incomprehensible soever it may appear to our fallible senses? To this end, do we from our hearts invoke His holy Name, saying, "LORD, I believe; help Thou mine unbelief"

Special Temptations. 79

(S. Mark ix. 24), "LORD, increase our faith"? (S. Luke xvii. 5.)

In temptations against hope, when the Evil One strives to persuade us that we have sinned beyond redemption, that the measure of our iniquity is full, and that we can expect neither grace nor mercy, have we called to mind the boundless Goodness of GOD, His Love, which desires that all men should be saved, and His Promise, which cannot fail, that He will never reject those who turn to Him with sincere repentance?

In temptations against purity, do we resolutely fly all occasions of sin, and are we careful to keep our thoughts employed upon holy things, especially in meditations upon the Passion of our Divine Redeemer, saying with S. Bernard, "How can my mind dwell upon worldly pleasures when I think of my GOD hanging upon the Cross?"

In temptations against charity, do we try to arouse in our minds the love of our neighbour, and the desire of serving him, remembering that all Christians are brothers, forasmuch as they are children of the Church of GOD, and members of the Body of our LORD JESUS CHRIST?

In temptations against humility, do we try to practise some mortification calculated to bring down our proud thoughts? Do we remember that honour is due to GOD alone, and that we have no right to glory in any thing? "O LORD, righteousness belongeth unto Thee, but unto us confusion of faces" (Dan. ix. 7).

In temptations against obedience, do we call to mind the great inward peace in which those live who are truly obedient? Do we remember that no sacrifice is so acceptable to GOD as that of an humble, obedient heart which has wholly renounced her own will?

Lastly, have we endeavoured to follow the counsels of the Saints of GOD, by making use of the following remedies against temptations: love of poverty against covetousness, prayer against discouragement, abstinence against gluttony, faithfulness to rule against laxity, and the spirit of retirement against worldliness?

THIRD POINT.

O MY GOD, Thou dost permit us to be tried in divers ways for the welfare of our souls, and Thou sufferest our temptations to be multiplied, in order that we may win a brighter crown: strengthen us therefore, we pray Thee, by Thy grace, that we, using well all those means which Thou dost bestow upon us for the overthrow of these our temptations, may at the last be enabled to say with Thine Apostle, " Thanks be to GOD, Which giveth us the victory through our LORD JESUS CHRIST" (1 Cor. xv. 57).

Of the Employment of our Time.

FIRST POINT.

LET us adore our LORD JESUS CHRIST, Whose death obtained for us the gift of time wherein to work out our salvation, although, for our sins, we deserved not this respite. Let us humbly give Him thanks for this great boon; but let us also be filled with a salutary fear when we remember the strict account which we must render to Him of the manner in which each one of these dearly-bought moments has been passed — moments which, perhaps, we have thoughtlessly squandered. Is there not here cause sufficient for apprehension on our parts?

SECOND POINT.

LET us now examine how we have employed our time, and let us see whether we have not, in point of fact, thrown away the larger portion of that which has been already granted to us. For time may be lost in various ways, as—

Firstly. When we do nothing—spending our lives in a state of bodily and mental inaction; such as is the case with many, whose lives are passed apparently in a dream, filled with projects impossible to realize, and with impracticable theories.

Secondly. Time is lost when it is ill-employed; as when it is spent in the society of evil-disposed or frivolous persons, or in gossiping and tale-bearing, in oppressing the poor, or in any way infringing the laws of GOD and of His Church.

Thirdly. We lose our time when we go through our daily duties, or our ordinary actions—such as meals sleep, conversations, or visits—simply from a human poin of view, and without referring them to GOD.

Fourthly. We even throw away our time when we spend it in good works which GOD does not require from us in the situation in life wherein He has placed us. As, for example, if a Priest having a cure of souls should retire from his post in order to devote himself more exclusively to meditation and prayer ; or if a servant should spend whole days in church instead of obeying his master's orders ; or if a youth in training for Holy Orders should imagine himself called upon to undertake parochial work and to instruct others, instead of implicitly following the directions of those placed in authority over him ; or if a magistrate, instead of administering justice, should visit hospitals and watch by the sick.

Fifthly. Time is also lost by those who perform pious and charitable works from any other motive than the love of GOD and the desire to promote His Glory.

Lastly. Those who fulfil all the duties demanded of them by GOD, lose their time if they do not perform them exactly at the period, in the place, and under the circumstances required by Him.

THIRD POINT.

O MY GOD, I know that time is brief, that its duration is uncertain, and that its loss is irreparable. How much reason have I to lament the manner in which I have hitherto spent it. Through Thy Grace, O LORD, I now make a firm resolution to employ better. that portion which still remains to me—that precious portion of time which Thy Blood has purchased for me, and which is now granted to me by Thy mercy in order that I may, by repentance, obtain pardon for my sins, that I may draw down Thy Blessing, and that I may finally gain life everlasting.

Of the Peace of God.

FIRST POINT.

LET us adore the profound and unchanging peace in which our GOD dwells from all eternity: that peace which is the highest felicity of Heaven, and the heritage of the elect: that peace which GOD alone can shed abroad upon the earth, and communicate to His children. This is the peace which our LORD JESUS CHRIST brought down to us on the day of His birth as the first-fruits of His love to man—the peace of which the Angels' song gave the first glad tidings, "Glory to GOD in the Highest, and on earth peace" (S. Luke ii. 14). Let us pour forth our hearts in praise and thanksgiving for this priceless boon.

SECOND POINT.

SINCE GOD'S peace can never be found in conjunction with sin —for the Prophet tells us, "There is no peace, saith my GOD, to the wicked" (Isa. lvii. 21)—have we, by the Divine grace, rooted out sin from our hearts, and conquered all our evil feelings?

Have we not been too much depressed by the contemplation of our failings, our frequent falls, our manifold wants, and our wretchedness?

Are we not easily disturbed and provoked by trifles of almost hourly occurrence: as, for instance, when we are kept waiting— when we are contradicted—when we are obliged to repeat several times over what we have said—when those to whom we speak do not attend to what we say—or when what we say is turned into ridicule?

Do we receive with perfect acquiescence all the decrees of

GOD'S Providence, however contrary to our own hopes and wishes they may actually be[1]? And do we submit with equal readiness to our appointed trials, in what form soever they may be sent to us; whether bodily, as sickness, loss of position, or pecuniary misfortunes, or spiritual, as weariness, dryness or temptations?

Have we not been over-anxious about our future—fearing that we may come to want, and that we shall lack the necessaries of life?

Lastly, when we have felt ourselves at peace, have we been careful to search into it thoroughly, lest it should prove a false peace, grounded only upon our carelessness, indifference, and self-indulgence? "Every one dealeth falsely . . . . saying, Peace, peace; when there is no peace" (Jer. viii. 10, 11).

THIRD POINT.

O MY GOD, how good a lesson against worldly anxiety is the admonition which Thou didst address to holy Martha, whom Thou sawest "cumbered about much serving," although her solicitude sprung from her desire to receive Thee with due honour: "Martha, Martha, thou art careful and troubled about many things: but one thing is needful" (S. Luke x. 41, 42). From henceforward we will labour earnestly, Thy grace assisting us, to attain unto Thy peace: and that we may the more earnestly strive after it, do Thou, we beseech Thee, enable us fully to realize the great happiness of those who possess this Thy peace, and who impart it to others; for to them alone is it given to bear the glorious title of Thy children: "Blessed are the peace-makers; for they shall be called the Children of GOD" (S. Matt. v. 9).

---

[1] "Ill that He blesses is our good,
    And unblest good is ill;
And all is right that seems most wrong,
    If it be His sweet will."
                  F. W. FABER.

Of Christian Meekness.

FIRST POINT.

LET us adore the great Example of meekness—our Blessed Saviour—typified by the beautiful emblem of gentleness, "the Lamb." By this name S. John the Baptist pointed Him out to his disciples, saying, "Behold the Lamb of God" (S. John i. 36). This name He also took Himself to make known to us His loving mildness, "I was like a Lamb" (Jer. xi. 19). This virtue of meekness shone forth in Him throughout His life on earth; it extorted the admiration of His persecutors during His passion, and it was contemplated with wonder by those who beheld His death upon the Cross. Let us then follow this great Example which He gives us, and let us ever bear in mind His most sweet invitation, "Learn of Me; for I am meek and lowly in heart" (S. Matt. xi. 29).

SECOND POINT.

THOSE who possess the true spirit of Christian meekness have so completely subdued, through the Divine assistance, all feelings of anger and irritability, that they are never surprised into a loss of temper. They are not prone to take offence, nor are they of a suspicious, bitter, or unforgiving disposition. They do not yield to the temptation of making repartees, nor do they indulge in raillery calculated to wound others. They avoid, as far as possible, all subjects of contention; and if they are obliged to differ in opinion from others, they do so in a conciliatory manner, showing no undue warmth or hastiness. They never speak harshly, even when their duty calls them to administer a reprimand. They can be firm in cases where gentleness is of no avail; but their rebukes are always so tempered by mildness as to resemble the admonition of a kind parent, rather than the reproof of a stern master. Lastly, they are unselfish, kind, obliging, and courteous to all: and they are only severe and uncompromising towards themselves. Let us see whether these characteristics of Christian meekness are to be found in ourselves.

THIRD POINT.

O MY GOD, we learn from Holy Scripture that meekness is one of Thy most favoured virtues—one, of which Thou didst not only give us Thyself the most perfect Example, but to the practice of which Thou hast annexed great rewards. May Thy grace, we beseech Thee, O LORD, aid the resolution which we now make, faithfully to strive to acquire the virtue of meekness, that so we may one day obtain the blessing which Thou hast promised to all meek and chastened souls, "Blessed are the meek; for they shall inherit the earth" (S. Matt. v. 5).

Of Lukewarmness.

FIRST POINT.

LET us adore our LORD JESUS CHRIST thus expressing, in His Message to the Church of Laodicea, the abhorrence of the sin of lukewarmness which fills His sacred Heart: " Because thou art lukewarm, and neither cold nor hot, I will spue thee out of My mouth" (Rev. iii. 16). These words are very awful, and are calculated to inspire a salutary fear in the souls of the lukewarm. We here see that our LORD so utterly detests this sin, that He pronounces against it the penalty of rejection expressed in the very strongest terms—terms which would seem almost to imply exclusion from the Divine grace. Let us therefore humbly and earnestly strive to shun the great peril of a state of lukewarmness.

SECOND POINT.

LET us examine whether we are not of the number of the lukewarm, against whom GOD has recorded this sentence of rejection. The lukewarm man is neither wholly devoted to a life of virtue, nor is he utterly given up to sin: he has not sufficient strength of will to endeavour to attain, by the Grace of GOD, to the utmost measure of perfection of which he is capable; neither has he so stifled his conscience as to be able to sin without remorse. He would on no account swear, or steal, or bear false witness; he abhors gluttony, impurity, and all mortal sins; but he feels no scruple in giving currency to slanderous reports, if they do not seriously affect his neighbour's reputation; in fact, so long as he can contrive to keep within the boundary of venial sin, he continues sinning rather than be at the trouble of putting a constraint upon himself. As his standard of perfection is very low, he rarely makes any progress towards attaining it : he takes no heed of small things, and neglects the counsels which he receives ; and, not perceiving that he stands in need of repentance, his conscience remains perfectly tranquil, as though he had no cause for apprehension. He fulfils his religious duties with tolerable exactness, is regular in prayer and meditation, attends Divine Service, receives Holy Communion, and, from time to time, makes good resolutions, which he occasionally puts in practice : nevertheless he has many self-indulgent habits which he takes no pains to mortify, provided they do not actually imperil his salvation. He is humble when no one despises him, gentle and courteous with those who are personally agreeable to him, patient when he is not called upon to suffer, obedient when he is ordered to do what is pleasing to himself. He delights in spiritual reading when he meets with a book to his taste, or which excites in him devotional feelings. But if he meets with contempt or opposition, if any thing puts him from his usual habits, or if he experiences dryness or discouragement in prayer, he quickly shows that he has neither true humility, nor meekness, nor patience, nor charity. In short, without being consciously hypocritical or deceitful, he conducts himself in such a manner as to obtain, under favourable circumstances, a character for great devoutness and spirituality, whilst really possessing but the outward show of these virtues, " Having a form of godliness, but denying the power thereof" (2 Tim. iii. 5). Let us try ourselves by these tests, lest we ourselves be so unhappy as to fall into this miserable state of lukewarmness.

THIRD POINT.

O MY GOD, since to be lukewarm in Thy service is to be in a state most fearful and full of danger to the soul—a state which is the source of the greatest evils ; do Thou, we pray Thee, kindle in our souls the fire of Thy Divine love, whereby we may be purified from the sin of lukewarmness, and may be strengthened to serve Thee with that zeal to which Thine Apostle urges us, beseeching us to be "fervent in spirit : serving the LORD" (Rom. xii. 11).

Of the Examination of Conscience.

THE HIGH ESTIMATION IN WHICH THIS DUTY SHOULD BE HELD BY US.

FIRST POINT.

LET us adore our LORD JESUS CHRIST, Who has assured us by His Saints that no exercise is more necessary or more beneficial to the soul than the examination of conscience; the daily practice of which is, indeed, a great aid to holiness of life, and one which cannot be neglected without sin. Let us give thanks to Him Who "searcheth the reins and hearts" (Rev. ii. 23), and let us fully recognize how infinitely important is the duty of corresponding with His grace by ourselves searching our consciences, and thus crushing sin in the very germ.

SECOND POINT.

LET us now ask in what light we have considered the duty of self-examination.

Do we regard it as a great help towards the amendment of our faults, and as an occasion of putting in practice one of the chief rules which the Saints of GOD give for our advancement towards perfection?

Are we convinced that self-examination is absolutely necessary for us, as being a daily preparation for the Sacrament of Confession; not only by enabling us to attain an exact knowledge of all our sins previous to confession, but also by inspiring a sincere contrition, which, in the event of our dying suddenly, or in a place where we are unable to obtain the assistance of a Priest, may, by the Divine grace, be permitted to supply the place of that Sacrament?

Do we remember that our conscience, if we never examine it, or if we only examine it superficially, becomes like ground which is suffered to lie fallow, and which is quickly overrun with weeds?

Do we consider that self-examination lays the axe to the very root of sin, destroying evil inclinations as soon as they begin to show themselves, and thus preventing us from forming any bad habits?

Do we call to mind that many of the most hardened sinners have been converted by the practice of self-examination; that the Saints of GOD have advanced in holiness of life by the same means; and that the greatest masters of the spiritual life have found no surer guide for those whom they directed, than this salutary exercise?

Lastly, as an undoubted proof of our desire to be diligent in fulfilling this duty, do we practise it every day at a specified hour, and especially at night, as we are admonished to do by many devout men; notably by S. Chrysostom in his Commentary on the fourth Psalm?

THIRD POINT.

O MY GOD, if those to whom the management of great wealth is entrusted are so exact in balancing their accounts daily, knowing that they are answerable to their employers for every item of the expenditure, how much more are we bound to be strict in keeping the account of our conscience, since we are responsible to Thee, from Whom nothing can be hidden, for every moment, every thought, every action of our lives, and for all the graces which we have received from Thee. Therefore do I beseech Thee, O LORD, to enable me diligently to search my conscience day by day, in preparation for Thy Judgment: for as Thy servant, S. Chrysostom, has well said, "If thus we put ourselves to trial daily, we may with less fear stand at the last day before the dread Tribunal."

Of the Examination of Conscience.

THE MANNER IN WHICH THIS DUTY SHOULD BE PERFORMED BY US.

FIRST POINT.

LET us adore our Lord Jesus Christ, Who sees us as we really are, and Who knows all our sins with their accompanying circumstances. He beholds us in the light of His truth, and therefore He judges us with equity, and not as men do, who are deceived by appearances, and who are misled by their prejudices or by their partialities. Let us return thanks to our Loving Saviour, Who will impart to us, if we ask Him, some portions of this Heavenly light, whereby we may diligently examine our consciences, and thoroughly search out each hidden sin.

SECOND POINT.

Let us ask ourselves whether we take due care to inquire into the state of our conscience, and whether we observe all the rules which are necessary to make our self-examination valid.

Do we place ourselves, with all fitting humility, in the presence of God, adoring our Blessed Saviour as our Judge, and beseeching Him to enlighten us as to the number and the greatness of our sins—since nothing but the light of Divine grace can enable us to know them and to examine thoroughly into them without running the risk of recalling evil thoughts or of arousing sinful wishes?

Do we make strong practical resolutions for the amendment of our lives?

Do we endeavour to attain to the frame of mind in which we should desire to be found at the hour of our death?

Has our examination of conscience been made daily, without fail; and made, if possible, at a certain fixed hour of each day?

Do we ever omit or slur over any portion of our examination, in order to shorten the time allotted to this exercise?

Do we examine ourselves minutely, carefully marking the smallest fault, lest we should pass it over, recalling our conversations, our thoughts, and our various employments during the past day; and remembering to note the good which we have left undone, no less than the evil which we have actually committed?

Are we not apt to imagine that it is unnecessary and even wrong to be very minute in self-examination—believing that such minuteness has a tendency to produce scruples, and that it is, besides, unsuited to persons living in the world?

Has our examination been searching and severe?

Do we try to discover both the causes and the consequences of our sins?

Do we neither endeavour to justify ourselves nor to make excuses for our errors?

Do we resolutely shut our ears to the suggestions of self-love, which would fain gloss over all our faults?

Lastly, when, in order to acquire a virtue, or to conquer some sin, we are obliged to confine our examination to one subject in particular, do we not quickly grow weary, and lay down our arms before the battle is won, instead of following the example of the Psalmist, who says, "I have pursued mine enemies, and overtaken them; neither did I turn again till they were consumed"? (Ps. xviii. 37).

THIRD POINT.

O MY GOD, I know that Thou dost desire that I should strive after holiness of life; and, to make this great aim the easier of attainment to me, Thou hast given me the help of self-examination; should I not then be without excuse if I failed to fulfil this obligation? Grant, O Merciful LORD, that I may never be wanting in correspondence to Thy grace; but may I so profit by the constant practice of this duty, that I may thereby, as Thou designest, root out sin from my heart, and plant therein the seeds of all virtue; thus obeying the command which Thou gavest Thy Prophet, "To root out . . . . and to destroy . . . . to build, and to plant" (Jer. i. 10).

Of Confession.

HOW WE SHOULD PREPARE OURSELVES FOR THIS SACRAMENT.

FIRST POINT.

LET us adore our Blessed SAVIOUR filling the office, so beautifully ascribed to Him by His Saints, of the Physician of our souls. He it is Who comes to us "with healing in His wings" (Mal. iv. 2). He it is Whose Blood "cleanseth us from all sin" (1 S. John i. 7), and Who has given us the Sacrament of Confession as a means whereby we may wash away the stains which sully the robe of our Baptismal innocence. How wonderfully are His wisdom and love displayed in this remedy for sin, to bestow which upon us He spared not His own Life—"giving," as S. Augustine saith, "His Blood to be the medicine of the sick."

SECOND POINT.

LET us examine our method of preparing ourselves for this Sacrament.

When we are about to approach the tribunal of Penitence, are we as anxious to avail ourselves of it as a sick person is to take any remedy from which he expects a certain cure?

Have we not gone thither reluctantly, or from habit, or out of deference to the opinions of others?

Have we not omitted to go from sheer indolence, or because we chanced to be engaged in study, or busied in some pursuit more in accordance with our inclinations?

Have we not made our preparation hastily, desiring only to get over our Confession as quickly as possible?

How we should prepare Ourselves for this Sacrament.

Has not this hurried and imperfect preparation given rise to many scruples, subsequently, as to the validity of our Confession, owing to the probability of some sin having been left unconfessed?

Have we not passed over some important circumstances which we might have remembered had we allowed ourselves sufficient time?

Lastly, have we taken care to be very exact in our method of preparation—especially in endeavouring to excite a true feeling of contrition in our hearts, lest, when we find ourselves in presence of the Priest, we should be so absorbed in the effort of recounting our sins, as to be unable to experience a hearty sorrow for them?

THIRD POINT.

O MY GOD, when I remember that the benefit which we receive from the Sacrament of Confession is in proportion to the diligence of our preparation; when I reflect that the principal part of this preparation consists in a strict self-examination, and that negligence upon this point often causes the great crime of sacrilegious Confession; I must acknowledge that I have much reason for apprehension upon this point, lest I, too, should have fallen into this sin. May the fear which now I feel, O LORD, prove a salutary fear, and may it lead me to abhor from my heart all my previous negligences and omissions, and to apply myself henceforward with earnestness to the fulfilment of the duty of a careful preparation for this Sacrament; since, as S. Augustine has said, "Carelessness may change our wholesome medicines into deadly poisons, and may cause us to receive judgment where we seek for healing."

Of Confession.

CONTRITION.

FIRST POINT.

LET us adore our Blessed SAVIOUR in the Garden of Gethsemane, bowed down with a weight of sorrow and anguish such as none other ever felt. "Is it nothing to you, all ye that pass by? Behold, and see if there be any sorrow like unto My sorrow" (Lam. i. 12). He beheld mentally the fearful ravages of sin and its dire effects—the gates of Mercy shut—man turning away from His Maker to serve the great Enemy of souls; and as these thoughts filled His sacred Heart, the World's Redeemer, burning with zeal for His Heavenly FATHER'S service, and with love for our souls, was so overwhelmed with grief, that not only did tears flow from His eyes, but a sweat of blood issued from His Body. Let us sorrow with our suffering LORD in grateful thanksgiving for these tokens of His great love.

SECOND POINT.

LET us ask ourselves whether we feel a hearty sorrow for having offended GOD.

Does the contemplation of our sins fill us with horror, and make us really abhor them and repent of them? Is our sorrow sincere, and does it possess all the characteristics of a genuine contrition?

Firstly. Is our sorrow an *interior* sorrow—proceeding from a truly contrite and humble heart? Is it not merely the offspring of our imagination, which, so soon as we feel some slight compunction, would fain persuade us that we are sincerely penitent? Are we not satisfied with the mere verbal repetition

Contrition.

of acts of contrition, without taking care to see that our souls are really touched by the spirit of repentance?

Secondly. Is our sorrow a *supernatural* sorrow; that is, a sorrow inspired by the grace of the HOLY SPIRIT, and founded on the pure love of GOD alone, not on the fear of eternal punishment, or on the hope of eternal reward? Has not our detestation of sin been chiefly caused by a desire to shake off the burden of remorse and to pacify our conscience? Do we not hate sin, only because it is opposed to our worldly interests; or, as did many of the heathen of old, simply on account of its natural hideousness?

Thirdly. Is our sorrow an *intense* sorrow, greater than we should feel for the loss of reputation or of riches, or for any bodily affliction, even though it were of life-long duration?

Fourthly. Is our sorrow an *universal* sorrow, extending itself without exception to all our sins, to those, more especially, towards which we feel most strongly drawn, and from which we find it most difficult to free ourselves?

Lastly. Is our sorrow accompanied by a firm and sincere resolution to abandon sin, and, by an earnest and heartfelt desire—not a mere passing wish—that we may rather suffer death than offend GOD by the commission of a mortal sin?

THIRD POINT.

O ALL-MERCIFUL GOD, my own experience tells me how hard and stubborn is this heart of mine, but the light of faith shows me that Thy sacred Heart is most tender and full of compassion; and even when Thine anger is most justly roused against sin, the humbled and repentant sinner will ever find Thee ready to receive him. True contrition, however, can only be produced by the operation of the grace of the HOLY SPIRIT. In this my destitute state, I have no resource save in prayer to Thee. Behold me now, thus prostrate at Thy Feet, imploring, with humble confidence, Thy Grace. In the words of S. Augustine, I beseech Thee, O LORD, to "give to mine eyes a river of tears, to my soul a sincere and lively sorrow, and to my heart a spirit of perfect penitence."

Of Confession.

HOW WE MAKE CONFESSION OF OUR SINS.

FIRST POINT.

LET us adore our Blessed SAVIOUR demanding at the hands of His precursor S. John the same Baptism which was received by those sinners who came "confessing their sins," to be cleansed from the stain thereof in the waters of Jordan. Most wonderful is the spectacle of our Divine Redeemer submitting Himself to this Baptism of Repentance as though He had been a sinner, even as we are. He, the All-holy, the Sinless One, subjected Himself to this rite, which He needed not, in order that we might find in His humility grace to confess our sins, and strength to bear with joyful love the penance which is imposed upon us.

SECOND POINT.

A CONFESSION, to be valid, must be *humble, entire, simple,* and *truthful.* Let us examine whether all these conditions have been fulfilled in our confessions.

Firstly. Do we make our confessions *humbly,* kneeling at the feet of the Priest in the attitude and in the frame of mind of a culprit before his judge? Do we not go through the catalogue of our sins as though we were repeating a lesson by rote with perfect indifference, feeling neither shame nor sorrow? Are we not secretly inclined to take pride in some of our sins, and to look upon them as proofs of a noble and heroic disposition? Do we not try to make excuses for ourselves in the course of our confession, in order to avoid the shame of avowing ourselves guilty?

How we make Confession of our Sins.

Secondly. Are our confessions *entire*, and do we take care to acknowledge all our sins, how great or humbling soever they may be? Do we fully explain every circumstance connected with them; for instance, the number of times each has been committed, and the consequences to ourselves or to others?

Thirdly. Are our confessions *simple*, without superfluous words or circumlocutory phrases? Do we confess all sins of which we are certain *as certain*, and all of which we are doubtful *as doubtful?* Do we avoid all obscure or equivocating expressions which might puzzle or mislead our Confessor?

Fourthly. Are our confessions *truthful?* Do we declare all our sins without making the slightest attempt to disguise or to justify them, or to give them such a colouring as might serve to palliate them?

Lastly. Do we, in making our confession, steadfastly resolve to follow the counsels of our Confessor?

THIRD POINT.

O MY GOD, in how fearful a state is the soul which dares not avow all her sins in Confession. She may conceal them from the Priest, but she must reveal them in the presence of the whole universe at the last dread Day: she shrinks from the brief shame which awaits her at the tribunal of Penitence, and her portion will be overwhelming confusion before Thy Judgment Seat. Save me, O LORD, from falling into this miserable blindness, and aid me, I beseech Thee, by Thy grace, so fully and truthfully to reveal all my sins in Confession whilst time is still mine, that Thou mayest be pleased to blot them out eternally, and to absolve me wholly from them.

Of Confession.

SATISFACTION.

FIRST POINT.

LET us adore our Blessed LORD'S ardent desire to offer Himself up in satisfaction for our sins. For this end He came on earth, He was born in poverty, He led a life of trial and privation, and finally suffered a most cruel death; yet, whilst undergoing all the torments and the humiliations of His most bitter Passion, yea, even in the act of shedding the last drop of His precious Blood for us, He still yearned for fresh sufferings, if thereby He might more fully atone for our offences[1]. Almost with His last Breath the World's Redeemer said, "I thirst;" for He was consumed by His thirst for our salvation—that salvation which could only be won through the Sacrifice of the LAMB "Which taketh away the sin of the World" (S. John i. 29). How perfect a Model does the Spotless SAVIOUR thus afford to sinners who, filled, through His grace, with zeal for the execution of the Divine justice upon themselves, desire to make satisfaction for their sins,

[1] "Oh, generous love! that He Who smote
In man for man the foe,
The double agony in man
For man should undergo;
And in the garden secretly,
And on the Cross on high,
Should teach His brethren and inspire
To suffer and to die."
Dream of Gerontius.

Satisfaction.

"Always bearing about in the body the dying of the LORD JESUS, that the life also of JESUS" may "be made manifest in" their "body" (2 Cor. iv. 10).

SECOND POINT.

LET us now ask in what spirit do we accept and perform the satisfaction enjoined by our Confessor.

Firstly. Do we accept our penance submissively, receiving it as from our Blessed LORD Himself by the instrumentality of His Priest? When the penance imposed by our Confessor appears to us too severe, do we not murmur, instead of acknowledging that our sins deserve a far heavier penalty? Do we listen with attention and respect to the exhortations of our Confessor? Do we not sometimes disapprove tacitly of his counsels, or have we not even, occasionally, dared openly to oppose them? Do we interrupt him with questions, either from over scrupulousness, or impatience, or irreverence?

Secondly. Do we make a point of performing the penance enjoined as soon as possible? Have we not sometimes delayed doing so on various trivial pretexts? Do we perform it with great exactitude and devotion, and with a great desire to atone for having offended GOD? And do we, in performing it, unite ourselves with the sufferings of our Divine Redeemer, and place our sole trust in the merits of His Atonement?

Lastly. When we have accomplished our penance, have we not felt self-satisfied, as though nothing further remained to be done; instead of remembering that, even could we receive an assurance of never again falling into sin, we ought yet to do life-long penance for those sins which we have already committed?

THIRD POINT.

O MY GOD, I know that I owe satisfaction to Thee, Whom I have so grievously offended; and therefore I am bound to accept not only submissively, but joyfully, the sufferings which Thy Providence appoints for me, and the penances which Thou dost enjoin by the mouth of Thy Priest, who is Thine ambassador to declare unto me Thy will. I feel that my sins deserve far heavier penalties, which yet Thy great Mercy does not exact. Oh, give me grace, I beseech Thee, to take refuge in the Tribunal of Penitence which Thine infinite Goodness has established, and where Thou dost await us, not as our Judge, but as our Advocate and Mediator.

Of Direction.

THE NEEDFULNESS THEREOF FOR ALL MEN.

FIRST POINT.

LET us adore our LORD JESUS CHRIST in His dealings with S. Paul after his Conversion. The great Apostle only desired to know the Divine Will and to accomplish it : " LORD, what wilt Thou have me to do ?" And the Master, Who had that moment illuminated his mind with celestial light, and Who had poured out most abundant graces upon him, straightway uttered this command, " Go into the city, and it shall be told thee what thou must do." Then was the convert brought to Damascus, and placed under the direction of Ananias, who, in a vision, had been instructed by GOD Himself concerning this " chosen vessel," the appointed Doctor of the Gentiles. Thus may we plainly see that none ought to dispense themselves from obedience to these counsels of the HOLY SPIRIT, in which the needfulness of direction is so clearly inculcated : " Lean not unto thine own understanding" (Prov. iii. 5). "Obey them that have the rule over you, and submit yourselves ; for they watch for your souls, as they that must give account" (Heb. xiii. 17).

SECOND POINT.

LET us examine what our feeling has been concerning the needfulness of direction, and how we have acted in this matter.

Have we not erroneously supposed that to submit oneself to a Director was a comparatively modern practice, unknown in the earlier ages of the Church of GOD, notwithstanding the maxims and the personal examples which His Saints have afforded us upon this very point ?

The Needfulness of Direction for all Men.

Have we not tried to persuade ourselves that our own judgment would suffice to direct us—disregarding this saying of S. Basil, a Father of the Church, "No one, by himself, is capable of deciding what is best for himself"?

Have we not relied over confidently on the guidance of reason alone; not considering how fallible is this poor human reason, nor how many great intellects have been led astray through trusting in her-too implicitly?

Do we not also rashly presume to constitute ourselves judges in our own cause; to prescribe spiritual remedies for ourselves; or even to make choice of a career, or to decide upon a vocation for ourselves, without taking counsel of our spiritual guide?

THIRD POINT.

O MY GOD, Thy Saints have declared to us that a soul without direction is in no less peril than a ship without a pilot, than a blind man without a leader, or than a sick man without a physician. How then can I, knowing my own weakness, be so presumptuous as to imagine that I am competent to undertake the task of self-guidance? Preserve me, I beseech Thee, O LORD, from falling into so dangerous an error. May I ever remember the precepts which the great masters of the spiritual life have bequeathed to us on this head; and may I submit myself henceforward with trustful humility to the counsels of my Director, looking upon him as one appointed by Thee to lead me in the way of salvation.

Of Direction.

THE NECESSITY OF CHOOSING A SKILFUL AND PRUDENT DIRECTOR.

FIRST POINT.

NOTHING more clearly shows the great importance of circumspection in the choice of a Director than the counsel which the HOLY SPIRIT puts into the Mouth of the Son of Sirach, " Have but one counsellor of a thousand" (Ecclus. vi. 6). In the choice of secular friends, we may allow ourselves, within due limits, a certain latitude; some being commendable for one quality, some for another. But the selection of a Director is a matter requiring long and prayerful consideration: we must choose him "of a thousand," for our soul's health may depend upon our decision. Then, when once our choice is made, let us submit ourselves to him unreservedly; giving thanks to the HOLY SPIRIT, Who hath appointed him to watch over us, and to help us in our spiritual necessities.

SECOND POINT.

LET us examine how we have proceeded in choosing a Director.

When GOD has put into our hearts the desire of Direction, have we looked upon this desire as a great grace, to be received with gratitude, and to be acted upon without delay?

Have we implored the light of the HOLY SPIRIT to direct our choice in a matter of so much importance?

Have we not, on the contrary, been imprudent enough to choose a Director hastily, without sufficient knowledge of his qualifications for such an office?

Have we not cherished a secret hope that our Director might not prove a man of experience and discernment, lest he should possess too keen an insight into our weaknesses; that he might not be eminent for piety and zeal, lest he should too rigorously enforce the obligation of walking in that "narrow way" which is so hard to flesh and blood; that his standard of morality should not be evangelically pure and lofty, lest he should too sternly reprove our many lapses from the paths of virtue?

Lastly, do we reflect that if we choose a Director who is not enlightened and experienced, he may mislead us; that, if he is not devout and zealous, he may be careless of the state of our souls; and that should his moral standard be low, he will undoubtedly neglect our best, our eternal interests?

THIRD POINT.

O MY GOD, when I call to mind all the counsels of Thy Saints upon the immense importance of choosing a good Director, how rash should I be were I to make this choice hurriedly or unreflectingly. Aided by Thy Grace, I will shun this danger; being resolved to take no single step in this matter, without much prayer that Thy HOLY SPIRIT may vouchsafe to make known to me him whom Thou dost appoint to be the visible guardian of my soul. "Thou, LORD, Which knowest the hearts of all men, show whether of these . . . . Thou hast chosen" (Acts i. 24).

Of Direction.

HOW WE SHOULD BEAR OURSELVES TOWARDS OUR DIRECTOR.

FIRST POINT.

LET us adore our LORD JESUS CHRIST submitting Himself to His Ever-virgin Mother, and to S. Joseph: "He . . . was subject unto them" (S. Luke ii. 51). In His Human Nature, He reverenced them as invested with the authority delegated to them by His Heavenly FATHER; and, therefore, He, the Maker and Ruler of all things, fulfilled all their behests with a loving and filial obedience. Let us give Him thanks for having thus made the duty of following Direction so attractive to us; since in His prompt and cheerful submission, as in all things else, He has left "us an example, that" we "should follow His steps" (1 S. Pet. ii. 21).

SECOND POINT.

LET us now examine in what manner we have borne ourselves towards our Director.

Have we regarded his authority over us, as being of Divine appointment?

Have we with a lively faith obeyed the precepts of the Saints of GOD, by looking upon him "as an Angel of GOD . . . . . to discern good and bad" (2 Sam. xiv. 17); even as the Galatians looked upon S. Paul, "Ye . . . . . . received me as an Angel of GOD, even as CHRIST JESUS"? (Gal. iv. 14.)

Is it not owing to our forgetfulness of this holy rule that we are sometimes repelled by the manner of our Director—

that his counsels are repugnant to us—and that we are disposed to be scandalized, and to take offence at whatever he may say or do?

Have we not asked his advice from motives of curiosity, or of vanity, or of human respect, rather than from a desire to know the Will of GOD in our behalf?

Have we consulted him with perfect openness and confidence as a charitable physician, and a faithful friend given to us by GOD to assist us in our needs?

Have we disclosed our inmost heart to him without disguise or reserve; concealing no single thought, or wish, or aim, or temptation?

Do we faithfully obey his instructions according to the rule laid down by the Saints of GOD, "doing neither more nor less nor otherwise than he commands"? (S. Bernard.)

Lastly, to sum up all in few words, do we bear ourselves towards him with reverence; do we listen to him with entire confidence; do we speak to him with sincerity and openness; and do we obey him with faithfulness?

THIRD POINT.

O MY GOD, I know that in too many instances direction is unprofitable to us, because we fail to discern Thee in the person of the Director: may Thy Grace, therefore, I pray Thee, enable me ever to behold Thee in him whom Thou hast placed over me in things spiritual: that so I may follow the example of the saintly Anchorite who said that he experienced not the slightest difficulty in obeying the commands of his superior, how harsh and arbitrary soever they might appear to human nature, because he always beheld in him the Master, CHRIST JESUS.

Of Holy Communion.

OF PREPARING OURSELVES FOR HOLY COMMUNION.

FIRST POINT.

LET us adore our LORD JESUS CHRIST in the most Blessed Sacrament of His Body and Blood, wherein He desires to be mystically united to us. In order that we may dispose ourselves to receive Him in a fitting spirit, He repeats to us the loving and heart-stirring summons, " Behold, the Bridegroom cometh; go ye out to meet Him" (S. Matt. xxv. 6). How great is the goodness of our Blessed SAVIOUR in thus vouchsafing not only to come to us, but even to give us warning of the necessity of preparing ourselves for His reception. Let us pour out our hearts, our minds, and all our powers, in returning thanks to Him for these proofs of His boundless love.

SECOND POINT.

LET us examine in what manner we are accustomed to prepare ourselves for Holy Communion.

Firstly. Are we perfectly pure from all stain of mortal sin, the commission of which would cause us to make a sacrilegious Communion, and thus to be guilty of the Body and Blood of the LORD? Do we take care to be free from all inclination to venial sins, which are displeasing in the sight of GOD, and which prevent our receiving the fulness of His Blessing in Holy Communion? Do we detach ourselves, as far as possible, from all created things—since, if we regard them with inordinate affection, we put them in competition with our love of the

Creator, Who desires that we should give our hearts to Him, wholly and undividedly?

Secondly. Do we aim at perfect purity of intention; having for our only motives the Glory of GOD, the establishing of His Kingdom in our hearts, the corresponding with our SAVIOUR'S desire of making His abode in us, the revivifying of ourselves with His life, and the attainment of that blessed transformation which He prayed His FATHER to accomplish in His Disciples, and in "them also which shall believe on Me through their word; . . . . . . that they also may be one in Us"? (S. John xvii. 20, 21.)

Thirdly. From the first moment of our waking on the Day when we are to be admitted to the Sacred Banquet, do we feel a great desire to receive our LORD—a loving desire, like that of a child about to welcome his father—an ardent desire, like that of a hart panting after the water-brooks—a pure desire, like that of the Prophet-King, when he cried out, " Oh, that one would give me drink of the water of the well of Bethlehem"? (2 Sam. xxiii. 15.) S. Ambrose's comment on this passage is as follows: "David thirsted not for the element of water, but for the Blood of CHRIST."

Fourthly. Are we on the day of our Communion more recollected, more retired from society, less occupied with worldly business, than usual? Do we keep a strict watch over all our senses, especially over our sight; thus following the example of a great Servant of GOD, of whom S. Jerome tells us, "To his eyes, which sought CHRIST, nothing else appeared worthy of regard"?

Lastly, in order that we may not disregard external fitness in our solicitude for spiritual preparation, are we careful when we approach the Altar to be apparelled in a decent and suitable manner, neither over-studied nor negligent, and in accordance with our station in life?

THIRD POINT.

ALMIGHTY GOD, since we read that the foolish Virgins were shut out of the bridal chamber because their lamps were untrimmed; since the man who came to the feast without having on a Wedding Garment was bound hand and foot, and cast into the outer darkness; how can we dare to draw nigh to Thy Banquet without due preparation? May Thy grace, O LORD, mercifully enable me so to take warning by these examples which Thy Gospel affords us, that I may never be so presumptuous as to present myself at Thine Altar, without having previously complied with the injunction of the Apostle S. Paul, "Let a man examine himself[1], and so let him eat of that Bread, and drink of that Cup" (1 Cor. xi. 28).

[1] "It is a day of fear:
Rise up betimes, go forth alone
With tongue fast-sealed and heart bowed down,
    Because thy LORD is near.

"Leave not thy thoughts to roam
Hither and thither, where they would;
Lest fretful cares on thee should crowd,
    Forgetful of thy home.

"Let not thine eye go free;
Look on the earth beneath thy feet,
The pit that for thy sins was meet,
    Had GOD been just with thee.

"Bethink thee of thy sin;
A stifling cloud, a festering sore,
A rotting canker at the core,
    That gnaws thy heart within.

"Good art thou to the sight;
But would thy cheek be dry as now,
As gay thy smile, as bright thy brow,
    If all were brought to light?

"Yet not in gloomy sadness
Be thy heart bowed and eye downcast:
Is not the night of sorrow past?
    Is't not a morn of gladness?

"Think on the Holy Feast,
On His dear love and gracious Name
Who sanctifies Himself, the same
　　Both Sacrifice and Priest.

"Go, and be one with Him;
Dwell thou in Him and He in thee;
Him freely love Who sets thee free,
　　Though but in shadow dim.

"For it shall not be so
In that great day when faithful souls,
Whom flesh doth sway and sin controls,
　　As they are known shall know:

"To be for ever one
With Him, Whom with the FATHER High,
And SPIRIT, Angels tremblingly
　　Adore as GOD alone.

"Bless, LORD, Thy child, oh, bless;
Strengthen my weakness; soothe my grief;
Forgive and help mine unbelief;
　　Restore my faithfulness."

　　　　　　　　　　WILLIAM GEORGE TUPPER.

Of Holy Communion.

THE ACTS WHICH WE SHOULD MAKE TO OBTAIN THE GRACE OF A WORTHY COMMUNION.

FIRST POINT.

LET us adore the infinite Goodness of the SON of GOD, Who after having suffered death for us upon the Cross, gives Himself to us day by day in the Sacrament of Holy Communion. Therein He gives Himself to us utterly, without stint: He gives His Body, His Blood, His Graces, His Merits, His DIVINITY Itself[1]. In His great Love, He even, if we may so speak, lavishes Himself upon us. Must not the hardest heart become softened when this GOD of Love draws nigh, and must not its cold ingratitude give place to warm thankfulness for so marvellous a Grace?

SECOND POINT.

LET us examine whether we have faithfully made all the acts prescribed by the Saints of GOD, as being amongst the most efficacious means of obtaining the grace of a worthy Communion.

Firstly. Have we made an act of faith in the Real Presence of our Blessed LORD in the Eucharist, and are we firmly con-

---

[1] "Thy Body, Soul, and Godhead, all,
   O Mystery of Love Divine,
 I cannot compass all I have,
   For all Thou hast and art are mine!"
                                F. W. FABER.

vinced that hidden under the Elements of Bread and Wine, we worship the Maker and Ruler of the Universe, Who, being GOD from all Eternity, was made Man, and died upon the Cross for the salvation of all [2]?

Secondly. Have we made an act of humility upon the approach of our Divine Redeemer—acknowledging that we are most unworthy to receive the King of kings in our poor house of clay, and saying from our heart, with the Centurion, "LORD, I am not worthy that Thou shouldest come under my roof" (S. Matt. viii. 8), with S. Peter, "Depart from me; for I am a sinful man, O LORD" (S. Luke v. 8), and with S. John the Baptist, "Comest Thou to me?" (S. Matt. iii. 14.)

Thirdly. Have we made an act of the love of GOD—remembering that in this Divine Sacrament the Love of JESUS is most fully shown; since here He gives Himself to us as the Spouse of our souls, thereby constraining us to love Him with our whole soul in return.

Fourthly. In the act of reception, during the precious moments when our LORD comes to us, do we throw ourselves in entire dependence upon Him as the supreme Master of our heart—beseeching Him to accomplish His Will in us, and awaiting

---

[2] "O Godhead hid, devoutly I adore Thee,
Who truly art within the Forms before me;
To Thee my heart I bow with bended knee,
As failing quite in contemplating Thee.

"Sight, touch, and taste in Thee are each deceived;
The ear alone most safely is believed:
I believe all the Son of God hath spoken;
Than Truth's own word there is no surer token.

"God only on the Cross lay hid from view;
But here lies hid at once the Manhood too;
And I, in both professing my belief,
The same prayer make as the repentant thief.

"Thy Wounds, as Thomas saw, I do not see;
Yet Thee confess my Lord and God to be:
Make me believe Thee ever more and more,
In Thee my hope, in Thee my love, to store."

Hymn of S. Thomas Aquinas.—Translated by E. CASWALL.

from His Divine bounty, the miraculous change which He works in this mystery, "transmitting," as S. Augustine saith, "not Himself into us, but us into Himself"?

Lastly. Do we strive to bring ourselves into that devout frame of mind to which a great servant of GOD so admirably gives expression in his prayer on the Holy Eucharist? "Thee may my heart ever hunger after, and feed upon, on Whom the Angels desire to look; and may my soul be filled with the sweetness of Thy Savour. May it ever thirst for Thee, the Well of life, the Fountain of wisdom and knowledge, the Source of eternal light, the Torrent of pleasure, the Richness of the house of GOD: may it ever yearn for Thee, seek Thee, find Thee, tend towards Thee, attain to Thee, meditate ever upon Thee, and do all things to the praise and glory of Thy Name: and be Thou alone my Hope, my sole Trust, my Riches, my Joy, my Refuge, my Peace, my Help, my Wisdom and my Treasure, in Whom my mind and my heart are fixed and rooted firmly and immovably now and evermore. Amen."

THIRD POINT.

O MY GOD, when I remember that Holy Communion, which brings life and gladness to some, is to others the cause of misery and condemnation, I see plainly that these different effects are wrought in us according to the spirit wherewith we approach Thine Altar. Let this thought, O LORD, I pray Thee, be so fully impressed on my mind, that I may feel the dread of losing Thee no less than the desire of possessing Thee: thus may I ever in receiving Thee be filled with a lively faith, a deep humility, a burning love, a total abnegation of self, and a fervent longing to be wholly united to Thee in time and in eternity [3].

> [3] "Jesu, Whom for the present veiled I see,
> What I so thirst for, oh vouchsafe to me:
> That I may see Thy countenance unfolding,
> And may be blest Thy glory in beholding."
> *Hymn of S. Thomas Aquinas.*—*Translated by* E. CASWALL.

Of Holy Communion.

THE DESIRE WHICH SHOULD POSSESS US FOR FREQUENT COMMUNION.

FIRST POINT.

LET us adore the Eternal FATHER, Who, in His parental care for us, gives us His Beloved SON daily upon His Altars to become there the Food of our souls. Let us adore the SON, filled with the love of mankind, which urges Him to unite Himself to us in Holy Communion. Let us adore the HOLY SPIRIT Who, having none other will than that of the FATHER and of the SON, invites us to approach to the sacred Banquet. What heartfelt gratitude is due from us to the Three PERSONS of the Most Holy and Undivided TRINITY for Their loving solicitude in our behalf.

SECOND POINT.

LET us now ask ourselves whether we respond to our SAVIOUR'S earnest desire that we should often seek to draw nigh to Him in Holy Communion.

Firstly. Do we ardently long for the enjoyment of this great privilege, and do we rejoice when the day of our Communion approaches? Do we feel a great gladness when several festivals follow closely upon each other, and do we ask to be permitted to make more frequent Communions? Upon the day of our Communion, are our souls filled with that eager joy which the happy Zacchæus experienced when our LORD said to him, "To-day I must abide at thy house. And he made haste, and came down, and received Him joyfully"? (S. Luke xix. 5, 6.) Do we remember that, since our Blessed LORD in the Eucharist is called our Daily Bread, we ought, every day of our lives, to desire to receive Him, at least spiritually; and the effect of this desire should be made manifest in an increased purity of life, whereby we may become worthy to receive Him verily and indeed? "So live," says S. Augustine, "that thou mayest deserve to receive Him daily."

Secondly. When we have felt a desire for frequent Communion, have we carefully examined whether this desire was settled upon the true foundation, namely, the Love of GOD? Since, if it has its origin in any meaner motive—as spiritual egotism and vanity, or human respect—it resembles the excessive appetite for food which is sometimes engendered by disease, and which, far from being a favourable symptom, only fosters and increases the malady: in order to avoid this dangerous error, are we careful to regulate our wishes, as regards frequency of Communion, by the advice of our Director?

Thirdly. Instead of feeling this loving desire of frequent Communion, wherein we have the example of so many of the Saints of GOD, have we not been so unhappy as to experience an indifference, and even an unwillingness to share in this Heavenly Manna, this Bread of Angels? Have we not allowed festivals to pass over without our attempting to approach GOD'S Altar; and have we not secretly rejoiced when any obstacle arose to hinder our participation in the sacred Mysteries? Have we not abstained from Holy Communion either because the preparation took up more time than we liked to devote to it, or because we felt that more frequent Communion would lay us under the obligation of leading more saintly lives, and of keeping a stricter rule over ourselves than we were disposed to do?

Lastly. Under the pretence of doing greater honour to our Blessed LORD, and under a false appearance of humility, have we not tried to persuade both ourselves and others that too frequent Communions show a want of reverence for our Divine Redeemer in this adorable mystery?

THIRD POINT.

ALMIGHTY GOD, Who art the Bread of the Angels in Heaven, and Who dost vouchsafe to be the food of Thy faithful servants on earth; how happy are those blessed Spirits who are perpetually nourished by Thee, and who desire Thee the more they receive Thee. Do Thou, O LORD, we beseech Thee, fill us with the same holy ardour, that so we may taste Thy full sweetness when, responding to Thy gracious and loving invitations, we approach to the Heavenly Feast. "Come unto the marriage" (S. Matt. xxii. 4). "Eat, O friends; drink, yea, drink abundantly, O beloved" (Solomon's Song, v. 1) [1].

> [1] "Lord, to Thine Altar let me go,
> The child of weariness and woe,
>   My home to find;
> From sin, and sense, and self set free,
> Absorbed alone in love to Thee,
> Able to leave in liberty
>   This world behind.
>
> "Jesus, be Thou my Heavenly Food,
> Sweet Source Divine of every good,
>   Centre of rest;
> One with Thy heart let me be found,
> Prostrate upon that holy ground
> Where grace, and peace, and life abound,
>   Drawn from Thy breast.
>
> "There let me lean, and live, and lie,
> As fast the fleeting moments fly,
>   Sands in a glass,
> Which time may shake with restless hand,
> Yet only at Thine own command,
> Till to a dearer, happier land
>   My soul shall pass.
>
> "Then, then unveiled wilt Thou appear
> To those, who walking with Thee here,
>   These wilds have trod;
> In faith that with the Cherubim,
> The Saints, and hosts of Seraphim,
> They too may join the eternal hymn
>   To Thee, O God."
>
> M. BRIDGES.

Of Holy Communion.

THANKSGIVING AFTER COMMUNION.

FIRST POINT.

LET us adore our LORD JESUS CHRIST surrounded by His Apostles in the "upper room," joining with them in giving thanks to His Heavenly FATHER for the life-giving Mystery, which was instituted at the Last Supper. "JESUS took bread, and blessed, and brake it, and gave to them, and said, Take, eat; THIS IS MY BODY. . . . . . And He took the Cup, and when He had given thanks He gave It to them. . . . . . And when they had sung an hymn, they went out into the Mount of Olives" (S. Mark xiv. 22, 23. 26). With what a pure, tender, loving spirit of gratitude was our SAVIOUR'S sacred Heart then filled. How profoundly did His Human Nature annihilate Itself in the Divine Presence. How fervently did He pour Himself forth in prayer. How intense was His Love for His Eternal FATHER, and for all mankind. Let us render our homage of thanks and praises to our Beloved LORD and Redeemer.

SECOND POINT.

LET us examine how we spent the time allotted to our thanksgiving after Holy Communion :—

Firstly. Do we first of all adore our Blessed SAVIOUR, Who, being Very GOD of Very GOD, yet deigns to come and dwell in us? Do we humble ourselves to the dust in the Presence of our Heavenly Guest, Whose infinite Majesty can only be fittingly acknowledged by the most solemn Offices of Religion?

Secondly. Do we render Him thanks for His great Condescension in giving Himself to us? and considering on the one hand, the abundance of Graces which His Eternal FATHER bestows upon us through Him, and, on the other hand, our inability to give Him due thanks for all His bounties, have we begged of Him to supply what is wanting on our parts, and, Himself dwelling in us, to offer our tribute of gratitude to the Heavenly FATHER?

Thirdly. Do we give Him our undivided love in return for the great Love wherewith He hath loved us, and do we ardently desire to be inseparably united to Him now and for ever?

Fourthly. Do we open our hearts to Him unreservedly—disclosing to Him all our wants and all our sorrows, and making our petitions with the unbounded trust which a child feels in approaching its earthly parents? Do we remain for a time to meditate and pray, and to listen for the Voice of GOD speaking within us, as did the Psalmist; "I will hear what GOD the LORD will speak; for He will speak peace unto His people, and to His Saints; but let them not turn again to folly" (Ps. lxxxv. 8). Are we careful to make our thanksgiving, if it be in our power to do so, *before* leaving the Church where we have communicated—so as to prevent the wanderings of thought which might be occasioned by a change of scene, or by the lapse of any considerable interval of time? Have we not, on the contrary, sometimes, through carelessness, or indevotion, or over-eagerness about our worldly occupations, either deferred our thanksgiving or omitted it altogether? Have we not shortened our thanksgiving, or, if we have given the full time to it, have we not suffered our thoughts to go astray instead of concentrating them on the Presence of our LORD in our hearts? Have we whilst making our thanksgiving maintained a very reverential outward demeanour, kneeling in a humble, composed, and devout posture, and never lounging, or sitting, unless illness or infirmity make the latter position unavoidable?

Lastly. Have we offered ourselves, with all that we possess, to Him—beseeching Him to dispose of us according to His Divine will; since we are His absolutely, and to be used, if it be His pleasure, for His glory?

• THIRD POINT.

MOST Merciful LORD, from the bottom of my heart I do

Thanksgiving after Communion.

beseech Thee to pardon me for my many shortcomings in returning thanks for Holy Communion. I have indeed great reason to fear that herein may be found the cause of the small profit which I have hitherto received from my Communions. O my GOD, grant that I may henceforth shun this fatal carelessness which is the result of ingratitude—that hateful vice which, as S. Bernard says, "is as a parching wind, drying up the Fount of pity, the Dew of mercy, and the River of grace." O Infinite Goodness. Do Thou soften my stubborn heart and warm it with the fire of Thy love, that so, being moved by the contemplation of the priceless Treasure which Thou dost bestow on man in the Blessed Eucharist, my sole aim, for the future, may be to show my gratitude for this Boon. "Thanks be unto GOD for His unspeakable Gift" (2 Cor. ix. 15) [1].

[1] "Come, let me for a moment cast all earthly thoughts away,
And muse upon the sacred Gift which I received to-day.
This morning that Eternal Lord, Who is my Judge to be,
Came to this lowly tenement, and stayed awhile with me.

"With His celestial Flesh and Blood, my fainting soul He fed ;
With tender words of grace and love, my heart He comforted.
He, Who of all that live and breathe is all the Life and Breath,
This morning deigned to visit me in this my house of death.

"He, Whose immensity transcends Creation's utmost goal,
This morning deigned to be confined within my finite soul.
He, Who in endless wealth abounds, the world's Possessor blest,
This morning deigned, oh wondrous thought, to be by me possessed.

"He, Who in Awful Godhead sits upon His throne on high,
This morning entered my abode, in His humanity.
He, Who for me a trembling Babe, on Mary's breast reclined,
This morning in my heart and flesh His Deity enshrined.

"O Soul of mine, reflect, reflect ; consider, one by one,
What marvels of surpassing grace thy God in thee hath done.
His tender love with love repay, extol His sacred Name,
To all the world His greatness tell, His graciousness proclaim."
F. W. FABER.

Of Holy Communion.

HOW WE SHOULD DISPOSE OURSELVES TO ASSIST DEVOUTLY AND PROFITABLY AT THE CELEBRATION OF THE HOLY EUCHARIST.

FIRST POINT.

WHEN we are about to assist at the Celebration of the Holy Eucharist we should place ourselves in spirit with the Blessed Virgin on Mount Calvary, and there devoutly contemplate the LAMB of GOD offering upon the Cross the Sacrifice which He mystically renews day by day upon our Altars. Let us reverently endeavour to enter into the feelings which must have possessed the Virgin Mother's sword-pierced soul as she watched the death-pangs of Her Divine SON : so shall our eyes, wholly fixed upon our Dying LORD, refuse to be drawn aside by any outward object ; so shall our hearts, filled with the love of GOD, urge us to cast away all self-love, to crucify in ourselves whatever is displeasing to Him, and to be willing to sacrifice all for Him Who was slain for us, "that" we should "present" our "bodies a living sacrifice, holy, acceptable unto GOD" (Rom. xii. 1). Then let us, adoring the HOLY SPIRIT from Whom all good thoughts proceed, prepare to assist at the Celebration of the august Mysteries.

SECOND POINT.

DURING the Celebration of the Holy Eucharist we should endeavour to fix our thoughts upon one or more of the following subjects for meditation or intercession.

Firstly. The unbounded love of the Eternal FATHER Who

How we should dispose ourselves. 123

gave us His Only-begotten SON, and the infinite Goodness of the Divine SON Who gave Himself wholly to us.

Secondly. The various mysteries of the Life and Death of our Blessed LORD, as they are set forth in different portions of the office for Holy Communion [1].

Thirdly. Union of the people with the Priest in the Sacrifice which is now being mystically offered [2].

Fourthly. Our several necessities, as to which we implore the

---

[1] "O the Mystery, passing wonder,
  When reclining at the board,
 Eat—Thou saidst to Thy Disciples—
  That True Bread with quickening stored;
 Drink in faith the healing Chalice,
  From a Dying God outpoured.

"Then the glorious upper chamber
  A celestial Tent was made,
 When the bloodless Rite was offered,
  And the soul's true service paid,
 And the table of the feasters
  As an Altar stood displayed.

"Christ is now our mighty Pascha,
  Eaten for our mystic Bread;
 As a Lamb led out to slaughter,
  And for this world offerèd;
 Take we of His broken Body,
  Drink we of the Blood He shed.

"To the twelve spake Truth eternal,
  To the branches spake the Vine—
 Never more from this day forward
  Shall I taste again this Wine,
 Till I drink it in the Kingdom
  Of My Father, and with Mine."
   Hymn from the Greek.—Translated by J. M. NEALE.

[2] "He Who once to die, a Victim
  On the Cross, did not refuse,
 Day by day, upon our Altars,
  That same Sacrifice renews:

help of GOD through the merits of our LORD present upon the Altar.

Fifthly. The graces and blessings which we have received, and for which we desire to return thanks.

Sixthly. Union with the Church of GOD both Militant and Triumphant, sharing in intention her joys and sorrows, in accordance with the ecclesiastical seasons, and the commemoration of the day. Let us examine whether we have taken care to learn from our Director which of the above methods would be most profitable to our souls, and whether we have faithfully followed the counsels given to us upon this point. Let us also examine whether we have not allowed our thoughts to wander during the Celebration owing to sheer want of self-control; or whether these distractions be not caused by our coming to the house of GOD with our minds still occupied with worldly business, and our hearts disturbed by unchristian feelings.

Lastly. Let us ask whether we have assisted at the Celebration with an ardent desire of uniting ourselves to our Blessed SAVIOUR, especially at the moment when the Priest communicates; thus making a spiritual Communion, according to the fruitful practice of the Saints of GOD.

THIRD POINT.

O MY GOD, since the very Angels who wait around Thy throne rejoice to descend upon Thy Altars, and there to veil their faces before the Presence of the Spotless Victim, with what veneration ought not we, sinful dust and ashes as we are, to assist at these adorable Mysteries. O LORD, do Thou enlighten our minds, open the eyes of our souls, and increase our faith in this wonderful Sacrament; that so, when present at the Celebration of the Holy Eucharist, we may be inspired with a reverential awe like to that of the blessed Spirits who stand in Thy presence, evermore lauding and magnifying Thy glorious Name.

> While the people all uniting
>   In that Sacrifice sublime,
> Offer Christ to His high Father,
>   Offer up themselves with Him."
>   *Ancient Latin Hymn.*—*Translated by* E. CASWALL.

Of Penitence.

THE FIRST FRUIT OF PENITENCE, WHICH IS HATRED OF SIN.

FIRST POINT.

SIN is most hateful to GOD because it is wholly opposed to Him. "The LORD is far from the wicked" (Prov. xv. 29). He chastises sin whenever, wherever, and in whomsoever it appeareth, without favour or exception whatsoever. "Art thou he that shall altogether go unpunished? Thou shalt not go unpunished" (Jer. xlix. 12). Thus spoke the LORD by the voice of His Prophet to the unrighteous of old. Let us adore His justice, and, whilst fearing His chastisements, let us not fail to acknowledge His mercifulness and to love His holiness, and let us proclaim them to all.

SECOND POINT.

LET us examine whether we have felt that hatred of sin which true and perfect Penitence arouses in our hearts.

Do we remember that sin is the irreconcileable enemy of GOD, and that it caused the Death of our Divine Redeemer? And, looking upon it in this light, do we hold it in the uttermost abhorrence?

Do we hate sin as being the primary cause of all the ills which have afflicted the world since the disobedience of the first man?

Do we shun sin as the greatest of evils, since it alone can plunge us into eternal misery; and, therefore, it is more to be feared than the sharpest torments, or than death itself?

Have we been, on all occasions, willing to lose every thing or to suffer any extremity, rather than commit sin?

Do we wage war against it, attacking it in its inmost stronghold, by the daily crucifixion of our flesh, with all those evil inclinations which bring forth sin, for "sin, when it is finished, bringeth forth death"? (S. James i. 15.)

Have we also felt a great aversion from venial sin, and do we earnestly strive to avoid all those lesser sins into which we are most usually tempted to fall—such as slight deviations from truth in trifles, tale-bearing, sarcastic remarks, and, generally, all sins of the tongue?

Do we remember that we are the more bound to keep watch over ourselves in these apparently unimportant matters, since often that which is but venial sin in the eyes of the world, is mortal sin in the sight of GOD? Very frequently, too, the circumstances of our position in life determine the category in which the sin is to be placed; as, for example—a sin which might be venial if committed by a layman, if committed by a priest may become mortal on account of the scandal given thereby to the souls placed in his charge.

Lastly, do we endeavour to efface the traces left by sin, which the Saints of GOD call "the dregs of sin," so that no taint should remain to sully our minds or to tempt us back to our evil ways?

THIRD POINT.

O MY GOD, I acknowledge that sin is in truth the greatest and the most hateful of all evils: but I have much need of Thy grace to enable me to abhor sin utterly as it deserves to be abhorred. Grant me then, O LORD, I pray Thee, this grace, that so being filled with love of Thee, and detestation of sin, I may when assailed by temptation, repeat from my heart the words of the Patriarch, "How then can I do this great wickedness and sin against GOD?" (Gen. xxxix. 9.)

Of Penitence.

THE SECOND FRUIT OF PENITENCE, WHICH IS SELF-ABHORRENCE.

FIRST POINT.

LET us adore the Three PERSONS of the Most Holy TRINITY teaching us to abhor ourselves—that is, to hate "the body of this death" (Rom. vii. 24), the flesh which causes us to sin. The Eternal FATHER sentences the body to death and corruption: the Divine SON nails the body to the Cross, and commands all who would be His disciples to follow His example: the HOLY SPIRIT, Who dwelleth in us, wages unceasing warfare against the body. Let us, then, thank GOD for putting into our hearts the spirit of self-abhorrence, and let us, by a true penitence aspire to reap the full benefit of this grace.

SECOND POINT.

LET us examine whether we hate our bodies as all true penitents are bound to hate it.

Do we acknowledge that our bodies deserve chastisement as having so often rebelled against GOD, and as perpetually labouring to stifle the voice of the HOLY SPIRIT speaking within us?

Have we rejoiced when our bodies have been subject to hunger, to cold, and to sickness—knowing that these things are but the tithe of what we deserve to suffer for our sins?

Do we keep a rigid watch over our bodies—giving them only what is absolutely needful to sustain them, and refusing them the smallest indulgence?

Second Fruit of Penitence: Self-abhorrence.

Lastly, being fully persuaded that our bodies are disloyal traitors to GOD, that they keep us from Him, and that, if not kept in strong check, they may be to us the cause of endless misery; have we striven to rouse within ourselves the penitential zeal of the Apostle, who said, "I keep under my body, and bring it into subjection" (1 Cor. ix. 27), and do we, longing to be freed from the chains of the body, cry out with him, "O wretched man that I am! Who shall deliver me from the body of this death?" (Rom. vii. 24.)

THIRD POINT.

O MY GOD, with my whole heart do I desire to obey the injunctions which Thou dost deliver to us in Thy Gospel, that we should hate our own lives in this world; but in order that I may never slacken in my desire to obey Thee, do Thou, I pray Thee, imprint in my mind the very words in which Thy command is given, as well as the blessed promise annexed thereunto. "He that hateth his life in this world shall keep it unto life eternal" (S. John xii. 25).

Of Penitence.

THE THIRD FRUIT OF TRUE PENITENCE, WHICH IS LOVE OF THE CROSS.

FIRST POINT.

LET us adore our Divine Redeemer coming upon earth to make atonement for our sins. He took up His Cross at His birth, He bore it without shrinking during the whole course of His mortal life, and He died thereon, of His own will, for our sakes. Does not the example of the Spotless Victim thus show us how closely the love of the Cross, and the desire of being purified from sin, should be united in us? Let us, then, with the penitent Magdalene, who "loved much," follow Him to the foot of the Cross, and beg Him to give us the grace to bear it daily after Him.

SECOND POINT.

LET us examine whether we are really filled with that love of the Cross which distinguishes all true penitents.

Do we feel an especial devotion to the Passion of our LORD? Do we love to dwell in thought upon this mystery, adoring our Blessed SAVIOUR nailed to the Cross as a sin-offering for the whole world? Do we from our hearts desire that the Cross should be held in honour by all mankind? Do we always speak of it with reverence, and do we make some devout ejaculation whenever we see a Cross? Do we frequently make the holy Sign of the Cross to sanctify our ordinary actions, and to inspire us with devout thoughts[1]? Or has not our love of the Cross been

---

[1] "Whene'er across this sinful flesh of mine
I draw the holy Sign,

restricted to these external marks of reverence, and have we not shrunk back when called upon to take it up ourselves?

When any trial is sent us—as the death of a relative or friend, the loss of worldly goods, sickness, or humiliations; when we are slandered or unkindly treated by others; do we rejoice in being permitted to share in the Cross of our Divine Redeemer, and to drink of His Cup—remembering that it is the Cross which has reconciled us with GOD, and that it is the tree of healing, the fruits of which are grace and virtue and life everlasting?

Have we not rather, been of the number of those timid souls who would fain be penitent without suffering any thing for GOD, and whose lives are passed in weak apprehension, and, where it is possible, in avoidance of pain? Has not the Cross been to us a stumbling-block, even as it was to the Jews, or, as to the Greeks, foolishness; since many worldlings esteem the endurance of causeless sufferings to be a mark of folly?

Lastly, instead of glorying and rejoicing in the Cross, as did the Saints of GOD, when we are called upon to suffer, have we not been as those of whom S. Paul speaks, "of whom I have told you often, and now tell you even weeping, that they are enemies of the Cross of CHRIST: whose end is destruction" (Phil. iii. 18, 19).

THIRD POINT.

O MY GOD, how far am I from being able to enter into the joy of Thine Apostle S. Andrew, when He beheld the Cross which he had so long desired, and which was to be the instrument of his martyrdom. Give me, I beseech Thee, some portion of the grace which Thou didst bestow upon him, that so, when crosses are sent to me by Thee, I may exclaim with him, "O blessed Cross, consecrated by the body of CHRIST, take me from amongst men and give me back to my Master, that He may receive me by thee, Who redeemed me on thee!"

> All good thoughts stir within me, and renew
>   Their slumbering strength divine;
> Till there springs up a courage high and true
>   To suffer and to do."   J. H. NEWMAN.

Of Penitence.

THE FOURTH FRUIT OF PENITENCE, WHICH IS PEACE OF HEART.

FIRST POINT.

LET us adore our Blessed SAVIOUR the Prince of Peace, Who left us that peace, by His Apostles, as a perpetual bequest. "Peace I leave with you, My peace I give unto you" (S. John xiv. 27). How beautiful is this peace, "the peace of GOD, which passeth all understanding" (Phil. iv. 7). May the contemplation of the loveliness of the Divine Peace incite us to greater love and reverence for our dear LORD Who purchased it for us at the price of His own most precious Blood.

SECOND POINT.

LET us examine whether we possess that peace of heart which usually accompanies a sincere penitence.

The soul which is filled with this peace, although she grieves deeply that she has offended GOD, is not cast down by the remembrance of her sins, but, laying them at the foot of His Cross, she continues in perfect tranquillity, undisturbed by scruples and undismayed by fears.

She is particularly on her guard against scruples, which are often a subtle temptation of the Evil One.

She gives no heed to the suggestions of her ghostly enemy, but in the midst of temptations and assaults of all kinds, she remains unshaken, like a rock against which the waves beat in vain.

This unruffled tranquillity enables her to judge calmly and

Fourth Fruit of Penitence: Peace of Heart.

soberly in all spiritual matters, so that she does not fall into religious despondency, nor is she liable to be carried away by religious excitement or unregulated enthusiasm.

This tranquillity, too, leaves her open to receive the impressions of Divine grace, and to yield unquestioning obedience to each inspiration of the HOLY SPIRIT: for only in this perfect obedience can we find true peace as well as that true liberty "wherewith CHRIST hath made us free" (Gal. v. 1).

Thus, being wholly in conformity with GOD'S holy Will, and placing her sole delight in serving Him, she enjoys on earth a foretaste, as it were, of the bliss of Paradise.

Lastly, as she gratefully acknowledges the inestimable boon of possessing this Heavenly peace, so she strives her utmost to retain it by frequent retreats, by renunciation of worldly joys, by self-denial, by earnest endeavour to avoid even venial sins, by the practice of good works, and by entire trust in GOD.

Let us see whether we possess these signs of the interior peace which true Penitence produces in the soul.

THIRD POINT.

O MY GOD, the inexhaustible Source of all good, we ask from Thee the grace of inward peace. "Give to Thy servants that peace which the world cannot give." Do Thou bestow it upon us, O LORD, that thus we may remain tranquil and undismayed in the midst of our enemies, and that by Thy grace, nothing may have power to withdraw us from Thy love, or to turn us aside from Thy service.

Of Penitence.

THE MEANS WHEREBY TRUE PENITENTS MAY DERIVE BENEFIT EVEN FROM THEIR FALLS.

FIRST POINT.

LET us adore GOD in His wonderful dealings with penitent souls, wherein His all-powerful goodness causes even their sins to bring forth fruit unto Eternal Life. S. Paul saith, "We know that all things work together for good to them that love GOD" (Rom. viii. 28): and S. Augustine, in his Soliloquies, meditating upon this passage, says, "Even sin itself is amongst these things that work for good to those who truly love GOD." It is most true that nothing is more hateful than sin in the sight of GOD: nevertheless, in the spirit of penitence the faithful soul is enabled to profit by her falls, and to turn them to account in the great work of salvation. Let us give thanks to our LORD JESUS CHRIST, to Whom we owe this great miracle of grace.

SECOND POINT.

LET us ask ourselves whether we have profited by our falls, as do those who are truly penitent.

Do our falls make us more humble, more convinced of our own weakness, our unstableness, and our utter wretchedness?

Do we mistrust ourselves more, and do we keep a stricter watch over ourselves?

Do we have more constant recourse to prayer, and are we more diligent in good works—striving to run more swiftly the race which is set before us, and desiring to show forth abundance of righteousness where before was "superfluity of naughtiness" (S. James i. 21): thus following the counsel of Baruch, "As it was your mind to go astray from GOD: so, being returned, seek Him ten times more"? (iv. 28.)

Do we take advantage of our falls to gain a more exact knowledge of our weak points, and thus—like the governor of a fortress which has once been surprised—to be ever prepared on the side whence we have most reason to expect an attack?

Lastly, has the contemplation of our sins inspired us with that "godly sorrow," which, as S. Paul saith, "worketh repentance to salvation" (2 Cor. vii. 10), and which spurs us on with greater diligence in the path of perfection? "For behold this selfsame thing, that ye sorrowed after a godly sort, what carefulness it wrought in you . . . . . yea, what indignation, yea, what fear, yea, what vehement desire, yea, what zeal, yea, what revenge" (2 Cor. vii. 11).

THIRD POINT.

O ALL-MERCIFUL GOD, who could believe that sin which renders us so displeasing in Thy sight, should yet by Thy grace become a means whereby we may raise ourselves to Thee? Yet this miracle is daily wrought in those true penitents who humble themselves in contemplating their transgressions, and who labour unceasingly to root out evil from their hearts. Grant to us also, O LORD, we pray Thee, the spirit of true penitence, whereby, as S. Augustine saith, "Our sins may become steps of the ladder by which we mount upwards.

Of Penitence.

THE PENITENTIAL SPIRIT.

FIRST POINT.

LET us adore our LORD JESUS CHRIST communicating to all the members of His mystical Body the true spirit of Penitence. This Divine spirit is the sole motive-power of sincere repentance: wanting which, it is in vain that we bring our bodies into the strictest subjection: but possessing which, the easy yoke of Christian self-rule becomes very precious in the sight of GOD. Let us give thanks to our Blessed SAVIOUR for admitting us to share in this heavenly spirit.

SECOND POINT.

HE who is filled with the penitential spirit never ceases to lament his sins, and, in the words of the Psalmist, his "sorrow is continually before" him (Ps. xxxviii. 17).

He looks upon himself as a criminal guilty of treason against the Divine Majesty: and he considers all the trials and sufferings, whether bodily or spiritual, with which he may be visited, as the just chastisement of his sins. Constantly desiring to suffer for his sins, he looks forward to death as being the appointed penalty of sin : but should it please GOD to prolong his days upon earth, he is grateful for the respite which enables him more effectually to prepare for the awful moment when, by the Divine grace, "that which was ordained to be the punishment of sin becomes a sin-offering," as S. Ambrose saith.

His zeal even makes him wish to suffer for others, especially for those over whom he may be placed in authority, or those to whom he may have proved a stumbling-block or a cause of scandal. This was the desire which S. Paul experienced, when he said to the Colossians, "I Paul .... now rejoice in my sufferings for you" (Col. i. 23, 24).

Lastly, always remembering that he is a member of the Body of CHRIST, he ardently longs to correspond with his Blessed LORD'S desire of suffering for His people—a desire shared by the Apostle, who in the Epistle above quoted goes on to say, "I .... fill up that which is behind of the afflictions of CHRIST in my flesh for His Body's sake, which is the Church" (Col. i. 24).

Let us now, therefore, inquire whether we have been filled in like manner with the true spirit of penitence.

THIRD POINT.

O MOST Merciful SAVIOUR, Thou wast pleased to suffer the penalty of our sins, treating Thy sinless self with unexampled rigour. Shall I, then, dare to spare myself, sinner that I am? Grant, O LORD, that I may never fall into this error: but may Thy grace fill me with the true spirit of penitence, whereby, in the humble confession of my sins, united with heartfelt contrition, I may, like the Prophet-king, find at once chastisement and healing. "For I acknowledge my transgressions: and my sin is ever before me" (Ps. li. 3).

Of Devotional Reading.

FIRST POINT.

LET us adore the goodness of GOD Who has inspired His Saints to bequeath to us, in their devotional writings, the fruits of their experience and their labours, whereby we may yet hold converse with them, and share in the light which the HOLY SPIRIT poured into their hearts whilst they lived on earth. Let us return thanks to Him for His great loving-kindness in thus watching over us, and providing for our every need.

SECOND POINT.

LET us now ask ourselves how we go through our devotional reading.

Do we set apart a certain portion of time daily for this holy exercise?

Before beginning our reading, do we ask GOD'S grace that it may be made profitable to us?

Are we careful as to the singleness of our intention—desiring only to correct our faults, to strive after what is good, and to advance in the way of holiness?

Are we not actuated by vanity—being very willing to talk of spiritual things, whilst shrinking from the effort of reducing them to practice: by love of novelty—thinking more of the style and language, than of the matter, of the book before us: or do we not set about it as a task—reading carelessly, without any real endeavour to derive benefit from what we read?

Do we try to retain, in part at least, the substance of what we have read, so as to make it the subject of our thoughts during the day?

Have we not read without method or order, and merely to please our own taste—just glancing over a book, and then throwing it aside for some other, instead of asking our spiritual Director to guide us in the choice of such as are most calculated to be of use to us?

Have we looked upon devotional reading as being a Heavenly Manna sent by GOD for the nourishment of our minds?

Does it not rather happen, from the disinclination which we feel for this exercise, that, as with bodily ailments, being unwillingly received, we can derive no benefit therefrom?

May not our want of inclination for devotional reading be partly caused by the too great pleasure which we take in secular reading, particularly in works of mere amusement, which, if indulged in without check, quickly destroy all relish for spiritual books?

Do we read attentively, without undue haste, and pausing from time to time to reflect upon those truths which have been most forcibly impressed on our minds?

Lastly, have we endeavoured to reduce to practice the great maxims of holiness of which we have been reading, thus—to quote from a Life of S. Ephrem—"our lives reflecting what the page records."

THIRD POINT.

O MY GOD, Thou hast shown us by the example of many amongst Thy Saints, how great are the graces which Thou dost bestow upon those whose delight is in reading of Thee and of Thy holy law: grant, I pray Thee, that I may take these examples to heart, and that nothing may ever tempt me to neglect a practice so dear to all who truly desire both to know Thy will, and likewise to do it.

Of Reading the Holy Scriptures.

FIRST POINT.

LET us adore the HOLY SPIRIT, the Guide and Inspirer of the sacred historians and prophets, whom He chose to record the great truths of the faith delivered to His Church. He is a GOD of infinite Goodness and Wisdom, Who, in condescension to our weakness, has been pleased to reveal Himself to us in the written Word, thereby to take possession of our hearts, and lead us to know and love Him to Whom we owe all. How happy are we to possess so priceless a jewel as the Sacred Volume, in reading which we become enriched with that knowledge which maketh "wise unto salvation" (2 Tim. iii. 15). Let us then render humble and hearty thanks to GOD, for this great treasure which He has been pleased to give into our hands.

SECOND POINT.

LET us now examine whether we have faithfully fulfilled the duty of searching the Scriptures, and whether we have done so in a fitting manner.

Have we read a portion of Holy Writ daily, with all the attention, reverence, and devotion, which we owe to the sacred volume?

Before reading, have we invoked the HOLY SPIRIT, beseeching Him to discover to us His hidden Wisdom, that we may understand the great mysteries concealed in the letter of His Word?

Has our intention been pure from all vanity and self-seeking, and has our only aim been to glorify GOD, and to know and do His will?

In all sorrow, discouragement, or depression, do we turn to

the Holy Scriptures for comfort, in accordance with the counsel of the Apostle, and the practice of the Saints of GOD?

Have we felt a special veneration for the New Testament, and do we always carry a copy of it about us, as S. Chrysostom relates was the custom amongst the early Christians?

Owing to our not being in a fitting frame of mind, and thus not remembering that it is GOD Himself Who speaks to us in His written Word, have we not felt a distaste for our Biblical studies; like S. Augustine, who, before his conversion, could not endure to read what appeared to him so simple and unadorned, when contrasted with the brilliancy and attractive elegance of profane authors?

Have we not been content to read GOD'S Word merely as an intellectual exercise, committing the text to memory, but not meditating upon the lessons which it conveys, or treasuring those lessons in our hearts, as did the Blessed Mother of our LORD? "His Mother kept all these sayings in her heart" (S. Luke ii. 51).

THIRD POINT.

O MY GOD, when I call to mind the command given by Thine Apostle to his disciple concerning the reading of the Holy Scriptures—"Give attendance to reading" (1 Tim. iv. 13)—when I remember all the testimony which Thy Saints have given us, as to the necessity and fruitfulness of this study, can I ever permit myself to neglect so great a duty? Suffer me not, O LORD, to be thus indifferent to Thy Word, but give me, I pray Thee, some portion of the grace which Thou didst bestow upon those great Saints and servants of Thine, who were unwearied in their searching of the sacred record, wherein they found unfailing beauty and sweetness.

Of Hearing the Word of God Worthily.

FIRST POINT.

LET us adore our LORD JESUS CHRIST, the Incarnate WORD, teaching His Disciples, by the Parable of the Sower, the duty of listening worthily to the Divine precepts. "The seed is the Word of GOD" (S. Luke viii. 11). How perfect is the instruction which our Master gives. He sets forth the power of the Word, He points out the various obstacles which hinder it from becoming firmly established in the heart of man, He shows the frame of mind in which it should be received. How wonderful it is that GOD Himself should deign to be our Teacher: but yet more wonderful is His goodness in giving us so many opportunities of profiting by His sacred teaching.

SECOND POINT.

LET us try ourselves by this Parable of the Gospel, that so we may judge how we have received the Word of GOD. Our LORD tells us, that His Word is the seed, and our hearts are the soil in which it is sown. Let us ask whether we are in a fit state to receive the visit of the great Sower.

Firstly. Are not our hearts like ground by the wayside, where the seed cannot spring up because it is trodden down and destroyed by the passers-by, and devoured by the birds of the air? That is to say, our hearts are hard, and the Word cannot prosper in them because they are given up to the things of this world, filled with the ideas of the age in which we live—perhaps even corrupted by evil inclinations: so that the Divine seed, being neglected, is quickly carried away.

Secondly. Are not our hearts like rock, where the seed sprang up and flourished, but, having no root, soon withered away? Is not this a true picture of our reception of the Word? We hear it without reluctance, nay, with gladness; but it makes a very slight impression upon us, and only penetrates the surface of our hearts. Some hidden defect, a remnant of self-love, self-will, self-confidence, these are so many rocks which keep the Divine Word from taking root; and therefore, at the first temptation, or the slightest difficulty, we are discouraged and fall away.

Thirdly. Or have not our hearts been like thorny ground, where, though the seed took root, it was speedily choked by the briars and weeds which grew with it, and hindered it from coming to perfection? Has not this been the case with us? Has not the Word of GOD been stifled in our hearts by earthly cares, by covetousness, by self-indulgence, by the desire of worldly distinction? And have we not reason to fear that these may cause us to fail in perseverance to the end, and so to bring forth no fruit unto life everlasting? Happy indeed should we be, if these hearts of ours were like the good ground of which our LORD speaks, and which represents those faithful souls, who "having heard the Word, keep it, and bring forth fruit with patience" (S. Luke viii. 15).

THIRD POINT.

ALMIGHTY GOD, when I consider the power and the sweetness of Thy Word, and, at the same time, remember how weak is my love for it, how little delight I take in hearing it, how superficial is the impression which it makes upon me, and how small is the extent to which I have hitherto profited by it; I cannot doubt but that the cause must be sought in my own coldness and indifference. Give me Thy grace, I pray Thee, O LORD, that I may resolve henceforth to be no unfruitful hearer. May I take to heart the lesson which Thou dost teach in this Parable; and may S. Augustine's memorable saying be often present to my mind, "He who neglects to hear the Word of GOD is not less guilty than one who, through carelessness, treats with irreverence the Body of the LORD."

Of our Daily Duties.

THE CARE WE SHOULD TAKE TO DISCHARGE THEM WELL.

FIRST POINT.

LET us adore GOD, the Maker and Ruler of all things, Who doeth all things well, Whose "incorruptible SPIRIT is in all things" (Wisd. xii. 1). In all His works, great and small, His perfection is made manifest. " In the Heavens," saith S. Augustine, " He has created Angels: on the earth worms and creeping things: yet is His infinite Greatness no less displayed in the one than in the other." Let us then with thankfulness acknowledge the perfection of all the works of our Heavenly FATHER, and let us endeavour to profit by the lesson which the Divine Master would have us take to ourselves—namely, that nothing in the circle of our duties should be great or small in our estimation, but that all should be discharged with equal thoroughness.

SECOND POINT.

THOSE who would faithfully acquit themselves of all their duties, should be in a state of grace : which is to say, that all must be done *in* GOD and *for* GOD.

Let us now examine whether we have sought to keep these rules.

Firstly. Have we kept a strict watch over ourselves, in order that we may, by GOD's help, attain and preserve this state of grace—remembering that all our works are dead, and unworthy of acceptance, unless they are done in the Name of our LORD and for His sake? Have we tried, in the discharge of our duties, to avoid, not only sin, but the smallest imperfection which might tarnish them in the sight of GOD?

Secondly. Have we not performed our duties with a divided attention, and, instead of thinking only of the work before us, have we not allowed our minds to wander—possibly imagining that we possessed intellects of sufficient capacity to entertain several subjects at once, forgetful of the saying of S. Gregory, "It is not to be wondered at if he whose mind is directed to many subjects at the same time often proves unable to master any single one"?

Thirdly. Have we offered up all our actions to GOD, to Whom they belong, and have we done so in an especial manner at the three periods recommended by S. Bernard—before beginning any work, in order to beg that the HOLY SPIRIT may enable us to do it well; whilst we are about our work, particularly if it should occupy much time, in order that the Divine Grace may strengthen us against all temptations which may intervene; and when our work is ended, in order that we may be preserved from all pride and vain-glory?

Lastly. Have we not failed in many of these points, more especially when our daily duties are of a commonplace and apparently unimportant character—forgetting how great an amount of grace we may draw down upon ourselves by doing well whatsoever our hand findeth to do?

THIRD POINT.

O ALMIGHTY GOD, give, we beseech Thee, to us Thy servants the gift of faithfulness, that so we may attain to holiness in this life, peace in the hour of death, and happiness in a blessed eternity.; and grant that these our actions may, by Thy grace, be so purified, as to become worthy offerings to Thee: for, "Whosoever offereth a sacrifice unto the LORD, it shall be perfect to be accepted" (Lev. xxii. 21).

Of our Daily Duties.

THE SPIRIT IN WHICH WE SHOULD DISCHARGE THEM.

FIRST POINT.

LET us adore our LORD JESUS CHRIST, Who in all His actions sought only to do the Will of His Heavenly FATHER, and to glorify Him. All the thoughts, words, and works of our Blessed SAVIOUR pointed to this end. "The FATHER hath not left Me alone; for I do always those things that please Him: I seek not Mine own glory" (S. John viii. 29, 50). Let us reverently adore the Single-mindedness of our Divine Redeemer, and humbly endeavour to imitate it.

SECOND POINT.

LET us examine ourselves as to the spirit in which all our actions shall be performed, so that in all things we may remember what, as Christians, we are bound to observe. Have we referred all our actions to GOD, and have we done all things in and for Him, in conformity with the great rule—that, as He is the First Beginning of all His creatures, so should He be their Final End and Aim?

Have we reflected that we depart from this rule as often as we act, not from bad motives only, but likewise from such as are in themselves neither bad nor good, or if we act without any special motive? To this end:—

Firstly. Have we, by the grace of GOD, banished from our minds all evil motives—doing nothing from pride or self-seeking?

Have we not been more desirous of fulfilling certain duties which were pleasant to us, rather than others which might be less suited to our inclinations?

And, in the discharge of these duties, has not our principal object been to gain the esteem and approbation of our fellow-creatures?

Secondly. Have we not been satisfied with ourselves, provided that our motives were not positively bad, or that they seemed good when judged by the standard of worldly morality?

Have we taken our meals and recreations, not with the object of gaining more strength for GOD's service, but simply for our own gratification?

Have we admired virtue only for its moral beauty, and have we been like those worldly persons who act well, and lead reputable lives, merely on moral or philosophical grounds?

Thirdly. Have we earnestly striven to avoid the chief snare of great regularity and constant repetition in the performance of our duties—namely, that of going through them as a mere habit, and without any special intention?

Have we asked of GOD the gift of good intentions, and when it has pleased Him to bestow this grace upon us, have we received it with fervent love and thankfulness, and has our prayer always been, that all which we do may be done to His Glory?

THIRD POINT.

O MY GOD, Who dost reject the greatest works which are not done with a single heart, and in a right spirit, and Who dost vouchsafe to accept and bless the very humblest offerings which are made for Thy sake and in honour of Thee; banish from my mind, I beseech Thee, all thoughts of any other than Thee, purify my heart from all trace of self-love, and fill it with the love of Thyself alone, that so, having no other aim but that of pleasing Thee, I may one day receive the reward which Thou hast promised in Thy Gospel to those who faithfully do Thy Will. "Blessed is that servant whom his LORD, when He cometh, shall find so doing" (S. Matt. xxiv. 46).

Of our Daily Duties.

THE NECESSITY OF REFERRING ALL WE DO TO OUR LORD JESUS CHRIST.

FIRST POINT.

LET us adore our Heavenly FATHER, Who desireth that His Divine SON should be the Example of all His faithful children. "For whom He did foreknow, He also did predestinate to be conformed to the Image of His SON" (Rom. viii. 29). And therefore He has given this Beloved SON to be the Governor and Guide, the Rule and Model, of our lives and actions. How great, then, is the debt of gratitude which we owe Him! For what more glorious calling can we have than to strive to live up to the pattern which CHRIST Himself has been pleased to give us?

SECOND POINT.

LET us examine whether we have referred all our actions to our LORD JESUS CHRIST, by seeking to follow in His steps, by casting ourselves entirely upon Him, and by uniting ourselves in spirit with Him.

Firstly. Have we earnestly sought to follow in the footsteps of our Blessed LORD, Who has vouchsafed to be our Model? Have we kept our minds constantly fixed upon the thought of our Divine Example, so as faithfully to print His Image in our hearts, in order that our lives may be, as it were, reflections of His Life on earth—"that thus," as S. Bernard says, "all our thoughts and actions may be directed to JESUS"? Have we meditated, not in a cursory manner, but dwelling upon each particular separately, upon the conduct of our Divine Redeemer in every circumstance of His Life—how perfect His obedience to His FATHER—how great His love and charity to all men—how strict His self-denial—how deep His abhorrence of sin—how entire His renunciation of the world? Have we endeavoured, through His grace, to imitate Him in each and all of these points?

Secondly. Have we thrown ourselves in utter dependence upon our SAVIOUR, knowing that we must do all things by His SPIRIT, and in His strength? Have we renounced ourselves and our own will, acknowledging our own blindness and weakness: and have we been content to feel that we are as clay in His hands, or as the body which is lifeless and motionless, save when stirred by the soul within?

Thirdly. Have we united ourselves spiritually by prayer to our dear LORD, beseeching Him that His infinite Merits may supply all our defects, and may make our efforts, poor and feeble as they are, worthy of acceptance? Have we, when tempted to neglect this practice, called to mind the words of S. Paul, "I can do all things through CHRIST, Which strengtheneth me"? (Phil. iv. 13.) And have we remembered that the Church of GOD offers all her prayers in the Name of CHRIST JESUS our LORD? And do we also remember that this is the great devotion of the Angels and Saints in heaven, who, in union with the Spotless LAMB, join in His perfect worship before the Throne of GOD? "A great multitude stood before the Throne, and before the LAMB, and worshipped GOD, saying —Amen. Blessing, and glory, and wisdom, and thanksgiving, and honour, and power, and might, be unto our GOD for ever and ever. Amen" (Rev. vii. 9. 11, 12).

THIRD POINT.

O ETERNAL GOD, Who desirest to be glorified through Thy dear SON, and Who delightest only in the homage which we offer Thee in His Name, grant that we may be filled with His

SPIRIT, that so He, working in us, and making us to be of one mind with Him, may enable us to render Thee the honour, praise, and glory which are Thy due, and which through Him alone can be well-pleasing to Thee.

Of our Daily Duties.

SOME HELPS GIVEN US TO ENABLE US THE BETTER TO DISCHARGE THEM.

FIRST POINT.

LET us adore our LORD JESUS CHRIST Who is pleased, in divers ways, to help us in every action of our lives, if we ask His assistance, to enable us to acquit ourselves well. He watches over us as a kind Father, taking care that nothing shall be wanting to aid us in the attainment of holiness. He loves us, but He would have us become worthy of His love by serving Him faithfully in the way which He has appointed for us. Shall we not have cause to be ashamed if we, bearing the glorious title of His children, do not obey the behests of our Just and Loving FATHER by doing the work which He has set us to do?

SECOND POINT.

LET us examine how we have used the four helps which our LORD gives us to sanctify our ordinary actions.

The *First* is, the practice of realizing the Presence of GOD: "As ye have therefore received CHRIST JESUS the LORD, so walk ye in Him" (Col. ii. 6).

Have we called to mind, whenever we were about to do any thing, that GOD was present, surrounding us on every side, penetrating the inmost recesses of our hearts, reading our most secret thoughts, knowing us as we can never know ourselves, and with His all-seeing eye beholding every circumstance, small and great, of our lives?

The *Second* is, that we should perform every action as if it were to be our last.

Have we seriously considered that each action of our lives may be the last which we shall be permitted to accomplish, and that therefore, in order not to be taken unawares, we ought to set about it as if we were well assured that it would be the last?

Have we sought to be like the faithful servants in the Gospel, watching for their LORD'S return, "that when He cometh and knocketh they may open unto Him immediately"? (S. Luke xii. 36.)

The *Third* is, to meditate upon the strict account of all our actions which we must render to GOD.

Have we remembered that all our thoughts, words, and deeds, small and great, will be passed in review before the dread tribunal of our Maker?

Have we considered that we may be found wanting, like the unjust steward, when his Master demanded the "account of" his "stewardship"? (S. Luke xvi. 2.)

Have we remembered that those who receive more graces than others, will have a stricter account to give: and that we, who, by our calling, are set apart for the service of GOD, having been more especially favoured, must be prepared for a more rigorous sentence if we have been unfaithful to our trust?

The *Fourth* is, the contemplation of the rewards and punishments allotted to our actions.

Have we reflected that the unending joys and glories of Paradise will be our reward, if we have done well that which was given us to do, as the everlasting darkness will be our portion, if our task has been neglected?

And have we remembered that our actions will be judged, not according to their actual importance or insignificance, but as they have been well or ill done?

Lastly, have we, in all difficulties, looked upon these four aids which our LORD has given us, as the most strength-giving means to which we can have recourse?

THIRD POINT.

O MY GOD, I am deeply grieved when I consider how little use

I have made of the efficacious means of grace which Thou hast given me to enable me to sanctify all my actions; even the humblest of which might have been ennobled by faithfulness in performing it: whereas, through my negligence, the highest have become unworthy. O Merciful LORD, grant that I may henceforth reap more benefit from Thy manifold goodness, and suffer not, I beseech Thee, that what Thou givest as a source of more abundant grace, should be, for me, a cause of greater condemnation.

Of Mental Prayer.

HOW THIS DEVOUT EXERCISE SHOULD BE VALUED AND LOVED BY US.

FIRST POINT.

LET us adore our LORD JESUS CHRIST, Who, in prayer, as in all things else, has left us an All-perfect Example. This holy exercise was to Him refreshment and rest. He could not worship His FATHER in the Eternal and Divine Life, being equal to the FATHER in all things: but He stooped for a time to the life of earth, and was made Man, that thus He, too, might offer His homage at the foot of the Everlasting Throne. Let us lovingly and reverently meditate upon His fervour in prayer: from the first moment that He drew mortal breath His Life was a prayer: His zeal never relaxed whilst He remained on earth; and now that His Visible Presence is no longer amongst us, He dwells, both in Heaven and on our Altars, a Suppliant for us to His FATHER: "now to appear in the Presence of GOD for us" (Heb. ix. 24).

SECOND POINT.

LET us now examine ourselves as to the manner in which we show our esteem and love for prayer.

Firstly. Do we remember that prayer is a privilege worthy of being exercised by the holy Angels themselves?

And do we reflect how great is the favour shown by GOD to us, unworthy as we are, in permitting us to come thus before Him, and to speak with the Almighty Himself?

In all temptation, sorrow, or weakness, do we fly to prayer as a sure refuge, an unfailing remedy, and an abundant source of all good gifts?

Do we go to prayer not only willingly but joyfully, and are we grieved at any interruption to our devotions?

Over and above the prescribed hours for prayer, which we are bound to observe, have we, in accordance with the recommendation of the Apostle that we should "pray without ceasing" (1 Thess. v. 17), been careful to do all things in a prayerful spirit, that is, with a raising up of our hearts to GOD, with a perfect realization of His Presence, and with the full purpose of doing His Will?

Secondly. Have we not sometimes deferred our prayers and meditations from indolence or disinclination, or from being busied about something which we liked better? and have we not, subsequently and in consequence, been careless and cold in our performance of these devout exercises?

Have we not been of the number of those who, without scruple, waste the greater part of their time in idle and unnecessary discourse, yet who seem to grudge the few moments that they spend in prayer?

Do we remember that, although we may be under the necessity of devoting some portion of the day to study, we are not thereby excused if we neglect prayer: nay, we have more need of meditating prayerfully upon the truths of our holy Religion, so as to be enabled to set forth her precepts in our lives, than of pondering them deeply with a view of giving verbal explanations to others?

Thirdly. When we have omitted our daily meditation, have we not sought to excuse ourselves by alleging a great pressure of business, as though we could have any business so important as that of prayer, which alone is capable of drawing down the Divine Blessing upon all our undertakings?

THIRD POINT.

O MY GOD, how can I wonder that I am so poor and destitute of all virtue, so powerless to resist temptation, so cold and indifferent in the performance of my duties, since I set so little value on prayer, since I am so lax in rendering Thee thereby the tribute due to Thee, and since I so reluctantly have recourse to it in all my needs? O Divine SAVIOUR, I acknowledge how faulty I have been: give me, I pray Thee, Thy grace that I may henceforth no more neglect this sacred duty, but that I may ever keep in mind the Example which Thou hast been pleased to give me herein, the loving urgency with which Thou dost invite me to it, and the great rewards which Thou hast promised thereunto: "Hitherto have ye asked nothing in My Name. Ask, and ye shall receive" (S. John xvi. 24).

Of Mental Prayer.

HOW WE SHOULD PREPARE OURSELVES FOR MEDITATION.

FIRST POINT.

LET us adore the infinite Goodness of GOD, Who, in His great Loving-kindness, desiring to communicate Himself to us in prayer, wills that we should with care prepare our souls that so they may be in a fitting state for the reception of His graces. These graces He showers down abundantly and bestows freely upon all who prepare themselves as He would have them to do: but He will not open His Treasure-house to those too-confident souls who tempt His anger, persuading themselves that they may gain all things by prayer offered up without due preparation. Let us then, whilst adoring His Goodness, humble ourselves in the Presence of His Justice.

SECOND POINT.

LET us examine whether we have with due care prepared ourselves for prayer and meditation.

Have we withdrawn our minds from all disturbing circumstances which might tend to make our prayer ineffectual?

Have we diligently purified our consciences, mortified our inclinations, and repressed all wanderings of thought?

Have we not, on the contrary, given the rein to our ill-temper and caprice, to our self-will and self-indulgence?

Have we not been too fond of hearing and repeating news, and is not a large portion of our time passed in frivolous or worldly conversations?

Do we feel ourselves really drawn to the retirement, recollectedness, and silence so essential for mental prayer?

When the hour of prayer is near, do we make a rule of reading no letters, save in cases of absolute necessity, and of avoiding general conversation, lest our minds should be diverted from the subject which alone should occupy us at such times?

Do we select some point in our meditation upon which to fix our last thoughts before sleeping, and to which we may recur as soon as we awake?

Have we taken care to adopt some approved method of mental prayer, to make ourselves acquainted with all rules which have been laid down for our guidance, to confide freely all our difficulties to our spiritual superiors, and to follow trustfully any counsels which they may give us?

THIRD POINT.

O MY GOD, since Thou hast Thyself taught us that unprepared prayer is but a tempting of Thy displeasure; since we know by our own experience that want of preparation is the most frequent cause of our shortcomings in prayer; and since Thy Saints have instructed us that the fruit of prayer depends upon the thoroughness wherewith we prepare ourselves, and that a worthless preparation is followed by an unanswered prayer; grant us, we beseech Thee, Thy grace, that so we may never be found in an unfitting state to make our supplications to Thee.

Of Mental Prayer.

THE PREPARATION: WHICH IS THE FIRST PART OF THE MEDITATION.

FIRST POINT.

LET us adore our LORD JESUS CHRIST Who in His agony prayed to His FATHER, kneeling and prostrate on the ground. Let us contemplate our Blessed Redeemer in this humble posture, and let us with awe behold His perfect annihilation of Himself in the Presence of the Divine Glory. How deep should be our feelings of shame at the thought that we, who are but dust and ashes, vileness and sin, have hitherto taken our LORD'S Example so little to heart.

SECOND POINT.

THE first part of Meditation is the Preparation; to which end we place ourselves in the Presence of GOD, we unite ourselves to our LORD JESUS CHRIST, and we invoke the help of the HOLY SPIRIT. Let us now examine how we have acquitted ourselves on these points.

Firstly. How do we place ourselves in the Presence of GOD?

Do we strive to bring before us with a living faith, the reality of the Divine Presence?

Do we reflect seriously upon the duty which we are about to fulfil, and upon the infinite Greatness of Him to Whom we address ourselves?

Do we, when kneeling down to pray, endeavour to fill our hearts with feelings of true devotion, and do we make the holy

Sign of the Cross with full trust in the efficacy with which GOD'S grace endows it against the assaults of our ghostly enemy?

Do we adore the Sovereignty of the LORD of lords with the most perfect reverence and entire humility?

Secondly. How do we unite ourselves in spirit to our LORD JESUS CHRIST?

Do we acknowledge ourselves unworthy—both as created beings, and as wretched sinners—to appear before GOD, and do we confess this to Him, humbly, feeling abashed and covered with confusion in His Presence?

Do we endeavour to purify our hearts by making an act of contrition, so as to be in a fitting state for the reception of His grace, which He never refuses to the really penitent and humble-minded?

Do we then seek to unite ourselves to our LORD JESUS CHRIST, desiring to pray with Him and through Him—to be clothed with His Righteousness—to ask nothing save in His Name—and to appear before the FATHER with Him for our sole Advocate and Mediator?

Thirdly. How do we invoke the help of the HOLY SPIRIT? Are we fully persuaded that we cannot of ourselves either offer up a prayer, or make a good resolution, or even entertain one single devout thought: and do we therefore readily renounce all confidence in our own reason, which is but blind and subject to error? Do we invoke the HOLY SPIRIT humbly, beseeching Him to be in our hearts and on our lips when we pray, that so He may drive far from us all slothfulness and coldness, and enlighten the darkness of our minds?

THIRD POINT.

ALMIGHTY GOD, Who dost listen to the prayers of those only who present themselves before Thee clothed in the righteousness of Thy SON, and who address Thee in His Name by the inspiration of the HOLY GHOST; grant me, I beseech Thee, Thy grace, that I may never presume to put up my prayer to Thee save in union with Thy Divine SON and the HOLY SPIRIT; so shall my petitions be favourably heard, so may I be permitted to be of the number of those who worship Thee " in spirit and in truth," from whom alone Thou wilt accept the tribute of praise and thanksgiving.

Of Mental Prayer.

THE SUBSTANCE: WHICH IS THE SECOND PART OF THE MEDITATION.—FIRST DIVISION.

FIRST POINT.

LET us adore our LORD JESUS CHRIST as the "Author and Finisher of our faith," and as the throne of GOD where the Eternal FATHER has placed Himself, not to judge, but to reconcile mankind. "GOD was in CHRIST reconciling the world unto Himself" (2 Cor. v. 19). There He is pleased to receive our homage; from thence He grants all, yea, more than all we ask; "Unto every one of us is given grace according to the measure of the gift of CHRIST" (Eph. iv. 7); from thence He showers down upon us His choicest blessings. How great is the happiness and sweetness of being thus constrained in all things to have recourse to JESUS! Let us render thanks for this grace a thousand-fold to our Heavenly FATHER.

SECOND POINT.

THE Substance of the Meditation, which forms the second part thereof, is divided under three heads; the first of which consists in the contemplation of our LORD JESUS CHRIST with reference to the subject chosen for meditation, and in the offering up to Him all our most important duties. Let us examine how we have acquitted ourselves under this head.

Firstly. Have we devoutly raised our minds to contemplate our Blessed SAVIOUR, and have we dwelt with great reverence upon His actions, His works, and all His teaching respecting the subject which has been appointed for our meditation? May we not have passed too lightly over this first part, either from not having accustomed ourselves to ponder lovingly upon every detail of our LORD'S Life, or from not giving due consideration to all which the Holy Scriptures relate of Him?

Secondly. After the lifting up of our hearts to the contemplation of our Divine Redeemer, do we offer our homage to Him as S. Augustine would have us to do, "Adoring, reverencing, praising, pleasing, loving, giving thanks, rejoicing"?

Do we *adore* Him, humbling ourselves at the thought of His infinite greatness, and of our own utter nothingness?

Do we *reverence* Him, giving ourselves up to all the feelings of loving wonder which should fill our souls, awed by the contemplation of that Perfection which we are unable to comprehend, even that of "the King in His beauty"? (Isa. xxxiii. 17.)

Do we *praise* Him, boldly setting forth His might, exerting all our powers in His service, and calling upon all creatures to join in honouring and worshipping Him?

Do we *love* Him, and do our hearts melt within us when we call to remembrance His goodness?

Have we no other aim but to *please* Him and to obey Him?

Do we *give thanks* to Him, and do we earnestly endeavour to show by our lives our gratitude for all His bounties?

Do we *rejoice*, in that He is All-perfect, possessing all the "treasures of wisdom and knowledge," and that "in Him dwelleth all the fulness of the Godhead bodily"? (Col. ii. 3. 9.)

THIRD POINT.

O LORD, Thou hast been pleased to give us Thy SON for "an example, that" we "should follow His steps" (1 S. Pet. ii. 21), and it is Thy will that we should strive to imitate Him in all things. We must, then, begin with prayer, which is one of our chief duties; grant, we pray Thee, that we may herein ever keep our minds fixed upon our Divine Model. Give us Thy grace, All-merciful FATHER, to the end that by constant meditation on the virtues which Thy SON came to show forth amongst us, we may be enabled to show our love for Him by practising them, and thereby conforming ourselves to His likeness.

Of Mental Prayer.

THE SUBSTANCE: WHICH IS THE SECOND PART OF THE MEDITATION.—SECOND DIVISION.

FIRST POINT.

LET us adore our LORD JESUS CHRIST, Who, in His boundless goodness, having been pleased to call us to the knowledge of His truth, in order that we may be living members of His Church and filled with His SPIRIT, desires that we should be of one mind with Him in all things. "Let this mind be in you which was also in CHRIST JESUS" (Phil. ii. 5). How great should be our happiness in being permitted to fulfil His desires by steadfastness in our calling! To this end let us ask His grace whilst we offer up to Him the duties and avocations of our state of life.

SECOND POINT.

UNDER the second head of the substance of our meditation, three points are to be insisted upon:—

Firstly. We must be fully convinced of the infinite importance of the virtue or of the article of faith upon which we are to meditate, and which we have above considered in reference to the example given us by our LORD and SAVIOUR JESUS CHRIST.

Secondly. We must feel that the subject chosen for meditation is one adapted to our own special needs.

Thirdly. We must earnestly beg of GOD that He will be pleased to grant us the grace upon which we now meditate. This is what is required of us in the present stage of our meditation. Let us examine how we have complied with the directions given to us.

I. In order more fully to impress upon our minds the vast importance of the subject of our meditation—whether it be upon an article of faith, or any particular virtue—have we weighed well all the arguments and opinions which have been authoritatively given on the subject? Have we not passed them over carelessly, alleging that we had a special love of the virtue in question, or that we felt no temptation to doubt the article of faith, and consequently, that it was not necessary for us to dwell long upon this point? Instead of making practical resolutions tending to the acquirement of virtue and the amendment of our faults, do we not enter into useless speculations, and feed our imaginations with subtle theories which only serve to nourish vanity, and which, in any case, are more fitted for the hours of study than for the time of prayer?

II. Have we duly considered the subject of the meditation with reference to our particular needs, remembering how much we lack of such a virtue, how weak we are upon such a point of faith? Are we truly grieved when we feel how far we are in all these things from the Spirit of CHRIST JESUS? Do we ardently desire to be conformed to Him, and do we earnestly beseech Him to enrich us with the virtue, or to give us a firm faith in the doctrinal truth, upon which we have meditated? And have we urged this request with perfect trust, with great humility, and with unflagging perseverance?

THIRD POINT.

O MOST Merciful and Gracious SAVIOUR, since Thy Light alone can give us full conviction of the truths upon which we meditate —can discover to us our own blindness and misery, or enable us to make our necessities known to Thee; fill us, we beseech Thee, with this heavenly Light, that by virtue of the same we may be firmly established in Thy faith, and may ever rule and order our lives thereby.

Of Mental Prayer.

THE SUBSTANCE: WHICH IS THE SECOND PART OF THE MEDITATION.—THIRD DIVISION.

FIRST POINT.

LET us adore the wondrous power and unshrinking courage which our Blessed LORD displayed in all that He undertook for His FATHER'S Glory. He devoted His Life to the work which His FATHER had given Him to do, He was content to endure hardness and humiliation—and, with the shame of the Cross in view, He went forward calmly to the end. The sorrows of death could not shake His constancy, and though the rage and cruelty of His enemies inflicted unutterable agony upon Him, He would not put the cup from His lips, but drank it to the dregs. And yet, with this example before our eyes, how weak, how vacillating are we—how readily do we turn back from the goal.

SECOND POINT.

THE forming of good resolutions is placed under the third head of the Substance of our meditation.

Let us examine how we have carried out this very essential portion of our exercise.

Have we not often made our mental prayer without following it up by any good resolve?

Have we not satisfied ourselves with vague and dreamy resolutions, which please the imagination without purifying the heart—which lull the remorse of conscience instead of rousing it to a sense of peril?

However earnest and sincere our resolutions may be, are they not often wanting in those characteristics which should mark all resolves formed during prayer with the intention of consecrating and sanctifying our lives?

Are these our resolutions *humble*, and accompanied by a great distrust of ourselves, and a perfect reliance on GOD?

Are they *courageous* and made in the true spirit of Christian courage, and do we ardently desire an opportunity of carrying them into effect, without counting the cost?

Are they *definite* resolutions, in which we clearly discern the time, place, and manner wherein we may be enabled to execute them?

Are they *practicable*, and of such a kind as to be put in action without loss of time; for, if once deferred, the opportunity may be lost, or even the resolutions themselves may be forgotten?

THIRD POINT.

O MY GOD, since even the holiest thoughts by which we are visited in prayer are fruitless, if they are not followed by good resolutions; and since the best resolves, if not carried into effect, do but render us more guilty in Thy sight; preserve us by Thy grace from forming any but such as we can put in practice; and grant that we may never fall into the miserable state of those who pass their lives in intentions and aspirations, which, however intrinsically excellent, can never, when unfulfilled, be pleasing in Thy sight. "The desire of the slothful killeth him; for his hands refuse to labour" (Prov. xxi. 25).

Of Mental Prayer.

THE CONCLUSION: WHICH IS THE THIRD PART OF THE MEDITATION.

FIRST POINT.

LET us adore the HOLY SPIRIT Who pours Himself out upon the Saints of GOD, teaching us from their lips and by their example, that it is the end—not the beginning—which crowns the Christian's course. This are we taught expressly in the words of Holy Scripture, which we may apply in an especial manner to the duty of bringing our prayers to a devout conclusion: "Better is the end of a thing than the beginning thereof" (Eccles. vii. 8). Let us receive this instruction with gratitude, and lay it well to heart.

SECOND POINT.

LET us ask ourselves whether we have diligently carried out all that is necessary to the right beginning, continuation, and ending of our meditation.

Firstly. Have we returned humble and hearty thanks to GOD for all the devout thoughts, holy affections, and other graces which He has vouchsafed to bestow upon us in prayer?

In seasons of dryness and lukewarmness have we not omitted to give thanks, believing ourselves to be passed over in the distribution of graces, and not remembering that we should count the honour of being permitted to address our LORD, as a favour far beyond our deserts?

Secondly. Do we grieve that our hearts have been so long closed against Him, and that we have so little corresponded

168 Conclusion: the Third Part of the Meditation.

with the inspirations of His Grace when it has pleased Him to grant it to us?

Have we lamented the little reverence which we have shown for His Divine Presence, and have we with great contrition asked Him to pardon our indifference, our wandering thoughts, our slothfulness, and all our other faults?

Thirdly. Have we carefully endeavoured to store up in our memories the pious thoughts and devout affections which GOD has been pleased to give us in Prayers—thus, to use an expression of S. Francis of Sales, gathering some spiritual flowers to refresh us with their fragrance amidst the toil and heat of our daily lives?

THIRD POINT.

O LORD, we know that in prayer the end is the crown thereof, since we conclude all prayer in the Name of Thy most dear-beloved SON: then, too, it is that from amongst the holy thoughts wherewith our minds have been filled, we make choice of those which seem most calculated to keep alive the flame of devotion, and to invigorate us in the performance of our duties. Give us, we beseech Thee, Thy grace, that we may firmly resolve ever to begin, continue, and end all our exercises of devotion as Thou wouldst have us to do, in a spirit of obedience to Thy will, and of childlike confidence in Thy love.

Of Mental Prayer.

THE BENEFIT WHICH WE SHOULD DERIVE FROM MENTAL PRAYER.

FIRST POINT.

LET us adore our LORD JESUS CHRIST in His Transfiguration, clothed with glory and shining with celestial brightness. Let us with wondering love contemplate Him as the Holy Gospel shows Him to us during His prayer on Mount Tabor; "And as He prayed, the fashion of His countenance was altered" (S. Luke ix. 29). As though He would thereby teach us how we, sinful as we are, may by prayer be transformed into the likeness of Him, the Sinless One. Who can be so hard of heart as not to be touched by the lovingness of this lesson?

SECOND POINT.

LET us now see how our prayer has profited us, and whether it has wrought any change in our lives.

In the *first* place, let us ask—Are we more recollected, and do we feel a closer union with GOD?

Are the motives of our actions purer and more single-hearted?

Have we a stronger abhorrence of sin, an increased reverence for holy things, more charity towards our neighbour, a stricter rule over ourselves, and a greater unworldliness of mind?

In short, what progress have we made in casting off the bonds of sin, and in striving to practise holiness of life?

Let us in the *next* place inquire what may have caused us to derive so little benefit from prayer, and why it is that this holy exercise, which works such miracles in the pure of heart, should make no apparent change in us?

Is it because we have too little love and esteem for prayer—only practising it because it is customary?

Is it because our hearts are too much absorbed by earthly attachments—so that we can give no share of them to GOD?

Or, *lastly*, is it that as soon as our prayer is ended we hasten back instantly to worldly conversation and occupations; we no longer think of GOD, nor do we dwell upon the devout thoughts with which He has inspired us; we forget all our good resolutions, and either do not seek for opportunities of putting them in practice, or allow such occasions as may occur to pass by unnoticed; and we take no pains to be more watchful over ourselves for the future?

THIRD POINT.

O MY GOD, how can it be that Prayer, which for others is so abundant a Fountain of Grace, should be as it were parched and dried up when I approach to it? How is it that I am so sunk in apathy and sloth, instead of being filled with love of Thee and zeal for Thy Service? Suffer me not any longer, I beseech Thee, O LORD, to presume upon Thy Mercies: but grant that, even though my heart should be still untouched by Thy Goodness, I may not be insensible to the dread warning of Thine Apostle: "The earth, which beareth thorns and briars is rejected, and is nigh unto cursing" (Heb. vi. 7, 8).

Of Mental Prayer.

THE WANDERINGS OF THOUGHT WHICH TROUBLE US DURING MEDITATION.

FIRST POINT.

LET us adore our LORD and SAVIOUR JESUS CHRIST praying to His FATHER—His sacred Heart and Mind being wholly absorbed in Divine Contemplation. " Mine eyes are ever toward the LORD," saith the Royal Psalmist (Ps. xxv. 15). How beautifully is this illustrated by our Blessed Redeemer, Who gives us herein the most perfect Example.

SECOND POINT.

Firstly. Let us examine the cause of our want of earnestness in prayer, and of the wanderings of thought which disturb our devotions. Do not these defects spring from our earthly affections—from the constant hurry in which we pass our lives—from our eagerness to hear and repeat news—from anxiety about our worldly affairs—from an unregulated love of study—or from too great indulgence in reading merely for our entertainment and pleasure?

Secondly. Let us inquire whether we have done all in our power to fix our attention, and to banish all disturbing ideas? When we are praying or meditating, do we, as soon as we find our thoughts are beginning to wander, turn ourselves with great humility to our Blessed SAVIOUR to ask His pardon, and then immediately revert to the subject of our meditation, without permitting our minds to dwell upon the idea which may have disturbed us?

Lastly. Have we earnestly begged of GOD the grace of keeping our hearts immovably fixed upon Him in prayer, being fully convinced that without His aid all our efforts must be fruitless, for "Except the LORD keep the city, the watchman waketh but in vain"? (Ps. cxxvii. 1.)

THIRD POINT.

GREAT GOD, I come before Thee humbled by the thought that till now I have never sufficiently realized the sinfulness of giving way to distractions in prayer, which not only show irreverence to Thy Presence, but which profane this holy exercise, and consequently render it fruitless. Grant that I may henceforth no more transgress in this wise, but that I may withdraw from all outward objects which might lead my thoughts astray—remembering the injunction which Thy Divine SON was pleased to give us on this head; "When thou prayest, enter into thy closet, and when thou hast shut thy door, pray to thy FATHER which is in secret" (S. Matt. vi. 6).

Of Mental Prayer.

DRYNESS AND OTHER TRIALS IN MENTAL PRAYER.

FIRST POINT.

LET us adore our LORD JESUS CHRIST in the Garden of Gethsemane and on the Cross of Calvary. There was His sacred Heart pierced with the sharpest sorrow—there did He suffer the extremity of desolation. Yet through it all, the Divine Redeemer continued to pray—yea, He prayed more fervently than before, to show us how we ought to bear ourselves when called to drink of His Cup. "And being in an agony, He prayed more earnestly" (S. Luke xxii. 44). Here, then, is our example. Happy is the soul which by faith can follow in His footsteps.

SECOND POINT.

LET us examine how we have borne ourselves when visited by dryness and desolation of spirit in prayer.

Have we not dwelt too much upon these trials, so as to be in danger of falling into a state of discouragement?

And instead of bearing them meekly, and with humility, as a means of self-mortification, have we not been disquieted and impatient—even to the extent of giving way to murmuring against the Divine Will?

Have we tried to discover the real cause of this dryness, so as to be enabled to apply the remedy?

Does it arise from our having allowed ourselves to be too much influenced by the spirit of the age in which we live, which causes us to seek for satisfaction in material things, neglecting to follow after spiritual things, and to have "our conversation in heaven"? (Phil. iii. 20.) In this case it behoves us strictly to deny ourselves all in which we have taken delight.

If it is sent by GOD as a special visitation—Have we made use of the means which have been employed by His Saints upon the like occasions?

Have we remembered that the wonderful gift of prayer possessed by some of the Saints of GOD, was, in many cases, bestowed as a recompense after long years of spiritual dryness?

Do we consider that this particular form of trial is often sent by GOD in His great loving-kindness towards us, to purify our hearts and prepare them for the fitting reception of His grace?

And lastly, do we reflect that GOD sometimes appears to withdraw Himself from us for a time, in order that we may thereby be moved to love Him more fervently, to seek after Him more diligently, to give ourselves up to Him more entirely?

THIRD POINT.

ALMIGHTY GOD, Thou seest my weakness and my want of courage to endure the trials which are sent me in prayer: suffer me not, I beseech Thee, to sink under them, however great they may be. Happy indeed should I be if I could follow the example of the Kingly Prophet, who, amidst darkness, dryness, and desolation, still put up his prayer to Thee with as much fervour as though he had been overwhelmed with spiritual favours. "My soul thirsteth for Thee, my flesh longeth for Thee in a dry and thirsty land where no water is: to see Thy power and Thy glory so as I have seen Thee in the sanctuary" (Ps. lxiii. 1, 2).

Of Christian Modesty.

FIRST POINT.

LET us adore our LORD JESUS CHRIST dwelling in His chosen servants, and endowing them with the great grace of Christian modesty—a grace which appears in their speech, in their demeanour, in every word and action of their lives. With this grace was His Virgin Mother most especially gifted: she, the purest of creatures, whom He chose to be His earthly parent, thus exalting her far above the Angels—she whom the Heavenly Messenger greeted as "highly favoured—blessed among women" (S. Luke i. 28), was pre-eminently distinguished by this virtue. In truth, it is one of the chief attributes of the children of GOD; insomuch that one of His Saints, S. Gregory Nazianzen, saith, "Where CHRIST is, there find we modesty." Let us beseech our LORD to bestow upon us this grace of modesty, which is so precious in His sight.

SECOND POINT.

THOSE who rightly esteem Christian modesty are so filled with reverence for GOD'S holy Presence, and with the fear of scandalizing His little ones, that they keep a constant and most careful watch over their conversation and demeanour. Let us examine how we have conducted ourselves in these respects.

Have we always kept in mind the great rule of S. Augustine —" That we should never suffer aught to appear in our speech, or in our bearing, which is inconsistent with the sanctity of the Christian profession, and with the edification which we owe to our neigbour"? This is also the counsel of S. Peter, when he beseeches those to whom his Epistle is addressed, to have their

Of Christian Modesty.

"conversation honest among the Gentiles : that .... they may .... glorify GOD in the day of visitation" (1 S. Pet. ii. 12).

Are we careful always to remember the Presence of GOD and of His Angels—since, as S. Paul tells us, "we are encompassed about with so great a cloud of witnesses"? (Heb. xii. 1.)

Do we call to mind the duty which we owe to our neighbour, of giving him an example of edification as our SAVIOUR has commanded? "Let your light so shine before men, that they may .... glorify your FATHER which is in Heaven" (S. Matt. v. 16).

Do we, in earnest, strive to banish both from our souls and our bodies aught which might prove a hindrance to us in the path of perfection whereunto, by GOD'S grace, we endeavour to attain—that we "may be holy both in body and in spirit"? (1 Cor. vii. 34.)

And, lastly, do we keep guard as carefully over ourselves, when we are alone, as though we were in presence of the whole world—knowing that we are bound so to do as being members of CHRIST, and habitations of the HOLY SPIRIT? This it is which S. Paul would have us call to mind when he says, "Know ye not that your body is the Temple of the HOLY GHOST which is in you, which ye have of GOD, and ye are not your own? For ye are bought with a price: therefore glorify GOD in your body, and in your spirit, which are GOD'S" (1 Cor. vi. 19, 20).

THIRD POINT.

O GOD of all Goodness, I know that, were we fully convinced of the excellence of Christian modesty, we should have no difficulty in accepting the maxim of one of Thy servants, that "no virtue is more fitting for a man—none more becoming in a Christian" (S. Bernard). Give me, I pray Thee, O LORD, a true love and esteem of this virtue, and grant that Thy grace may enable me to preserve it, throughout my life, with that faithfulness which is the distinguishing mark of Thy children.

Of being Poor in Spirit.

FIRST POINT.

LET us adore the HOLY SPIRIT thus instructing us, by the mouth of the Psalmist, to be poor in spirit; "If riches increase, set not your heart upon them" (Ps. lxii. 10). Let us with reverent and devout wonder contemplate the marvellous wisdom of this Divine teaching, which links together the two extremes of wealth and poverty, and thus enables us at one and the same moment to be both rich and poor—to be rich in graces though destitute of worldly possessions, and to be poor in spirit though abounding in material prosperity.

SECOND POINT.

HE who is poor in spirit is wholly detached from all the riches, honours, and pleasures of this world.

He weighs earthly possessions in the balance of the Temple, and by the light of the Gospel beholds their real worthlessness.

If he is poor, he strives to follow the example of the Apostles, and of the other Saints of GOD, who, having neither silver nor gold, yet made an ample offering of both to GOD, by never, for one instant, coveting either.

If, on the other hand, GOD has given him wealth, he looks upon himself as being but the steward thereof, holding it "as having nothing," and thus, in the words of the Apostle, "possessing all things" (2 Cor. vi. 10).

He does not talk of his riches with complacency, nor does he take pleasure in thinking of them, for his treasure is not in them.

He is not eager in the pursuit of wealth; he receives it with indifference, he bears the loss thereof with calmness.

He acts with perfect disinterestedness in all worldly business; and, remembering that he must render a strict account of the manner in which the goods entrusted to him by GOD have been employed, he is always ready to help those who are in need; he lends promptly, and he gives alms bountifully, without stint, ungrudgingly, as giving to GOD Himself in His poor.

Let us now see whether, on all these points, we have exercised ourselves in detachment and poverty of spirit.

THIRD POINT.

O MY GOD, I desire to be wholly detached from all worldly possessions: I renounce from my heart all my covetousness and love of riches: and, aided by Thee, I am resolved to practise that poverty of spirit which alone can enable me to become Thy true Disciple: for Thou hast said, "If thou wilt be perfect, go and sell that thou hast, and give to the poor, and thou shalt have treasure in heaven: and come and follow Me" (S. Matt. xix. 21). Enable me, then, I pray Thee, O LORD, to live a life of such entire detachment, as may show that, through Thy Grace, the possession of this world's goods is not incompatible with the cultivation of that poverty of spirit which Thou hast inculcated, and to which Thou hast promised so great a blessing. "Blessed are the poor in spirit: for their's is the kingdom of Heaven" (S. Matt. v. 3).

Of our Waking and Rising.

FIRST POINT.

LET us adore our LORD JESUS CHRIST taking upon Himself our human nature with all its infirmities, sin only excepted. He was weary and needed rest—He slept, and woke, and rose up to His daily task, even as we do. But all these actions were made holy by the spirit in which He performed them. In them He renewed that ardent desire to labour for the salvation of mankind which brought Him down from heaven on the day of His Incarnation; and He anticipated that fervent longing to be re-united to His FATHER wherewith He burst asunder the bonds of death upon the day of His Resurrection. Thus did our Divine Redeemer sanctify His rising up in the morning, and His nightly rest: let us, aided by Him, endeavour to begin each day as becomes His followers.

SECOND POINT.

LET us examine how we have demeaned ourselves upon our first waking in the morning, and in what frame of mind we have risen to set about our daily duties.

Do we, in the act of waking, give our first thought to GOD by offering ourselves wholly to Him and to His service?

Do we give Him our first word, by invoking the Name of the Most HOLY TRINITY, and our first action, by making the holy Sign of the Cross?

Do we remember that GOD delights to have the first-fruits of all His creatures, and that we are, therefore, bound to offer to Him the first actions of our day?

Do we rise promptly, with the cheerful readiness of a faithful servant who hears his Master call him to begin his daily work?

Have we not, from sloth and self-indulgence, remained in bed after we were summoned to rise?

Lastly, as soon as we have risen, do we perform our devotions in a reverential and loving spirit, begging our LORD to consecrate this day to Himself and to His service, offering to Him whatever we may be called upon to do or to suffer during the course of the day, and giving ourselves wholly to Him that He may strengthen us to live no longer for ourselves or for the world, but for Himself alone, being "dead indeed unto sin, but alive unto GOD through JESUS CHRIST our LORD"? (Rom. vi. 11.)

THIRD POINT.

O MY GOD, how can I be so heedless as not to strive after the sanctification of my waking and of my rising? How can I be so ungrateful as not to give to Thee, the All-bountiful, those first-fruits in which Thou dost delight? How can I be so blind as not to desire to perform well this first action of the day, on which so much depends? Grant, O LORD, that I may henceforth fulfil this duty in a devout spirit; and that I may be the better enabled so to do, make me ever to remember the counsel which Thou hast given by one of Thy servants: "Thy day, O Christian, will belong to whomsoever first takes possession of it; see, therefore, that thou give to thy LORD of the first-fruits thereof."

Of Conversation.

THE FAULTS WHICH WE SHOULD AVOID IN CONVERSATION.

FIRST POINT.

LET us adore our LORD JESUS CHRIST, dwelling upon the earth and conversing with men. How great was the grace which He thus conferred upon them. How holy were these conversations; how different from those which we hold—pervaded as they too often are by a spirit of malice and contentiousness—were the communications of Him, "Who did no sin, neither was guile found in His mouth." (1 S. Pet. ii. 22.) "He shall not cry, nor lift up, nor cause His voice to be heard in the street" (Isa. xlii. 2). Let us reverently contemplate our Divine Model.

SECOND POINT.

LET us ask ourselves whether we have taken due care to avoid those faults into which conversation most frequently leads us.

Have we shunned all calumny, falseness, and double-dealing?

Have we been careful to touch upon no subject which could recall the least shadow of evil?

Have no words of ours been prompted by feelings of vanity, anger, or contempt, or by the wish to wound others?

Have we indulged in mockery, especially against any persons who are uncongenial to us?

Have we ever permitted ourselves to speak lightly of sacred things?

May we not, by some careless or irreverent remark, have

deterred others from endeavouring to carry out the precepts of Religion?

Have we not spoken with too much warmth, and maintained our own opinion with too great a degree of obstinacy—thus falling into the "strifes" condemned by the Apostle: "The servant of the LORD must not strive; but be gentle unto all men"? (2 Tim. ii. 24.)

Have we introduced subjects of conversation which we knew were likely to lead to disputes, and upon which it would have been far better to keep silence?

Have we spoken in a manner contrary to holy charity, by criticizing the conduct of others, exaggerating their faults, depreciating their good qualities, embittering quarrels, or encouraging party spirit and divisions?

Have we not been so eager to hear ourselves speak, as to interrupt others, and do we not find ourselves unwilling to become listeners in our turn?

Lastly, has not our too great fondness for talking proved to us a fruitful source of wandering thoughts, tending to make our duties wearisome to us?

THIRD POINT.

O ALMIGHTY GOD, I know too well, by experience, how many and great are the dangers to be avoided in conversation, and how seldom we can escape unharmed. A word, or a look, may often cause a sin against brotherly love: pride and self-love are but rarely absent: the enemy of our souls spreads a thousand snares for us. O my GOD, I cast myself at Thy Feet, to implore Thy pardon for all the sins which I may have committed in conversation, and to ask Thy grace to enable me so to rule my tongue, that henceforth my "conversation" may "be as it becometh the Gospel of CHRIST" (Phil. i. 27).

Of Conversation.

THE VIRTUES TO BE EXERCISED IN CONVERSATION.

FIRST POINT.

LET us adore our LORD JESUS CHRIST, Who, in His intercourse with man, gave us the most perfect example of those virtues which it behoves us to exercise in conversation. He spoke with mildness; He listened with patience; He bore the defects of others with humility. How winning was His condescension. Nothing, says S. Augustine, can more fully engage our love and reverence than the contemplation of our Blessed LORD conversing with His people.

SECOND POINT.

LET us ask ourselves whether we, in our conversations, have been solicitous to exercise ourselves in those virtues which our LORD requires of us, and of which S. Paul speaks in his Epistle to the Ephesians, "lowliness and meekness, with long-suffering, forbearing one another in love" (Eph. iv. 2).

Firstly. Have we practised the virtue of *lowliness*—being deeply impressed with the sense of own unworthiness, and sinfulness, as compared with others? Have we shown due respect to all our brethren, as we are commanded to do by the Apostle, "in honour preferring one another"? (Rom. xii. 10.) Have we listened to others willingly, and have we deferred to their opinions instead of obstinately upholding our own as such? Have we borne with mildness any interruption? When tempted to say any thing which would be likely to obtain praise, have we chosen to keep silence rather than to speak?

Secondly. Have we practised *patience*—bearing with any weakness or defect in our neighbour, and showing no repugnance, however little pleasing his manner may be to us? When we receive any counsels for our spiritual guidance, pointing out to us our faults, do we receive them humbly, and without suffering ourselves to be ruffled in the slightest degree?

Thirdly. Have we exercised ourselves in *charity* and *forbearance*—showing in every possible way our sympathy with our brethren, and endeavouring to assist them in all their difficulties, to console them in their sorrows, to strengthen them in moments of weakness and temptation, and to speak always to them, and of them, kindly and lovingly? Have we sought to raise their minds to GOD by giving them holy counsels, filling their minds with the precepts of the Gospel, and arousing in them a devotional spirit? Have we, in a word, striven, after the example of the Apostle, to make ourselves all things to all men, in order to lead them to CHRIST?

Fourthly. Have we practised the virtue of *meekness*—seeking, as S. James says, to "show out of a good conversation" our "works with meekness of wisdom"? (S. James iii. 13.) Do we take in good part whatever may be said to us, personally? Do we try to put a favourable construction upon every thing; and, instead of justifying ourselves and condemning others, do we always endeavour to let any blame fall upon ourselves rather than upon them? In short, have we striven to show in our conversation lowliness, modesty, repression of self, holiness, zeal for the greater Glory of GOD, and for the salvation of our brethren?

THIRD POINT.

O LORD, how acceptable to Thee, and how profitable to our neighbours and to ourselves would our conversation be, if we endeavoured to find in it occasions for the exercise of those virtues of which Thy Divine SON gave us the example. May Thy Grace, O GOD, enable us so to walk in His steps, taking Him for our model and guide, that we may show ourselves to be in all things followers of Him, and especially so by having "our conversation" "in Heaven" (Phil. iii. 20).

Of Travelling.

HOW TO USE PROFITABLY THE TIME SO SPENT.

FIRST POINT.

LET us adore our LORD JESUS CHRIST, following Him in spirit in the various journeys which He had occasion to make during His life on earth. All were undertaken with a view to the fulfilment of His Mission: He sought only to obey His FATHER'S Will, and to do good to men. He "went about doing good" (Acts x. 38). Let us humbly offer our homage to this Divine SAVIOUR, Who so lovingly calls upon us to follow Him: "If any man serve Me, let him follow Me" (S. John xii. 26).

SECOND POINT.

WHEN, for sufficient reasons, and after due reflection, we have decided upon undertaking any journey, do we begin by recommending ourselves to GOD, to implore His All-powerful protection, and to draw down His Blessing upon us? And are we careful to leave all our affairs—especially such as are connected with our pastoral charge—in perfect order, so that as far as depends upon ourselves, our absence should cause no trouble or inconvenience to any one?

Have we not, whilst travelling, omitted our customary prayers and meditations, or have we not deferred them till the evening, when we were, perhaps, too tired to give proper attention to them?

Have we not been too ready to make our journey an excuse for not attending Divine Service on Sundays and Festivals?

Have we neglected no opportunity which may offer itself during a halt upon the road, of entering a church to return thanks to GOD for having conducted us so far in safety?

Have we not given ourselves up too entirely to the enjoyment of the moment, imagining that it was permitted us to regard the journey solely in the light of a recreation?

Have we been careful always to carry with us some devotional works; above all, the Holy Scriptures?

Do we suffer ourselves to give way to impatience at any accidental delay upon our journey, and do we murmur at the weather, the roads, or any trifling inconveniences which we may have to submit to, instead of being thankful and giving praise to GOD for whatever befalls us, as did the Kingly Prophet, "I will bless the LORD at all times"? (Ps. xxxiv. 1.)

Lastly, have we, under every circumstance, and in all things, so ruled our conduct as to be without reproach before GOD and men? "Giving no offence in any thing, that the Ministry be not blamed" (2 Cor. vi. 3).

THIRD POINT.

O ALMIGHTY GOD, we can have no more powerful incentive to regulate our conduct in our journeyings than the consideration that all which we do is done in Thy sight, for Thou dost "see my ways, and count all my steps" (Job xxxi. 4). Grant then, O LORD, that we may ever keep this thought present in our minds, and that, being thereby moved to keep a strict watch over ourselves, we may be of the number of those who find in every varying circumstance of life an opportunity of serving Thee, and who thus advance steadily in the ways of holiness. "The path of the just is as the shining light, that shineth more and more unto the perfect day" (Prov. iv. 18).

Of Retreats.

FIRST POINT.

LET us adore our LORD JESUS CHRIST, Who, after His Ascension, inspired His disciples with the desire of withdrawing themselves into the retirement of that " Upper Room," where, with the Blessed Mother of their Risen SAVIOUR, they "all continued with one accord in prayer and supplication" (Acts i. 14). Let us contemplate this Retreat of the Apostles, whence we may learn what is our duty when we would prepare ourselves to receive graces and favours from the All-bountiful. We must not be content merely to admire their devout fervour, but we must strive to imitate it.

SECOND POINT.

LET us examine how we have acquitted ourselves with respect to Retreats.

Have we felt all due love and esteem for this holy exercise, which is so healthful to the soul, and so essential for all who would make progress in inward perfection?

Have we made a rule of devoting a certain number of days in each year to this purpose, in accordance with the advice of the greatest masters in the spiritual life, and with the practice of all who earnestly desire to grow in holiness?

Have we not sometimes, through sloth or lukewarmness, omitted this duty—laying hold of some pretext of business, or work, or study, or infirm health, or other reason to excuse ourselves, and imagining that the time thus unlawfully abstracted from our devotions might be employed in some more practical manner?

At the same time, are we very certain that we do not make

our Retreats from a wish to stand well with others, or to gain credit for more than ordinary saintliness of life?

Before entering upon a Retreat do we, as far as possible, exclude from our minds all thought of our private affairs and secular business, and do we refrain from letter-writing and from all unnecessary conversations?

Are we actuated by a sincere desire of amending our faults and of establishing ourselves firmly in virtue, of rekindling our fervour of spirit, and of advancing in sanctity?

Have we been careful to do nothing from our own fancy and inclination, and have we strictly followed the advice of our spiritual superiors?

Lastly, has the close of our Retreat found us wholly changed from what we were in the beginning thereof; that is to say, more fervent in our love of GOD, more grateful to Him for all the graces which He has bestowed upon us, and more zealous in our resolutions to serve Him faithfully?

THIRD POINT.

O MY GOD, when I consider that it is in seasons of retirement that Thou dost communicate Thyself to us with most loving abundance, how must I reproach myself with my neglect of so holy an exercise! Henceforth let me resolve from my heart that this duty shall never be wilfully omitted by me. May Thy grace enable me to taste in it the sweetness which Thou dost promise us in the words of Thy Prophet: "I will bring her into the wilderness, and speak comfortably unto her" (Hosea ii. 14).

Of Self=discipline.

THE NEEDFULNESS OF THIS VIRTUE.

FIRST POINT.

LET us adore the HOLY SPIRIT, the source of all truth, impressing upon us by the mouth of His Apostle S. Paul, the necessity of self-discipline: "If ye live after the flesh, ye shall die: but if ye through the Spirit do mortify the deeds of the body, ye shall live" (Rom. viii. 13). Thus we see that upon self-discipline depends the salvation which we must work out with fear and trembling. Self-discipline gives health and life to our souls: the neglect thereof slays them. Let us receive this word with humility and meekness, and let us render our thanks and homage to Him Who has vouchsafed to impart it to us.

SECOND POINT.

SELF-DISCIPLINE is a grace whereby GOD enables His faithful children to bring the earthly part of themselves into perfect subjection.

Let us ask ourselves whether we have fully recognized our own great need of this grace. Have we looked upon it as an inseparable adjunct of the Christian life, and as a necessary means of promoting our growth in holiness? Have we remembered that no obligation is more frequently enforced in the Gospel than this of self-discipline?

When our Blessed LORD tells us that the violent take the Kingdom of Heaven by force; that he that hateth his life in this world, shall keep it unto life eternal; that we must deny ourselves and take up our cross and follow Him—what do all these sayings mean, but that we must be ever ready for suffering and self-sacrifice? This, too, is what S. Paul would have us to understand when he says, "They that are CHRIST'S have crucified the flesh" (Gal. v. 24).

Have we been fully persuaded that self-discipline affords great opportunities to all; to the sinful, of co-operating with the Divine Justice—to the Christian, of paying homage to the All-perfect Holiness—to the Priest, of offering an acceptable sacrifice to the Infinite Majesty? "Offer the sacrifice of righteousness," saith the Royal Prophet (Ps. iv. 5), for it is in such a sacrifice, the fruit of true humility and contrition, that, as we are assured in various portions of Holy Writ, the LORD GOD delighteth.

Are we convinced that, as the want of self-discipline is the origin of all evil, so the practice thereof is a very solid foundation whereon, by GOD'S grace, all good may be established?

Lastly, instead of taking to heart all which our Holy Faith teaches us concerning self-discipline, have we not suffered ourselves to fall into the too common error of the present age, which represents this salutary exercise as being supererogatory, and altogether unsuitable for those who are obliged to take an active part in the duties of life?

THIRD POINT.

O MY GOD, Thou wilt only receive those who come to Thee by the way of suffering and self-sacrifice. From this decree Thou wouldst not even exempt Thy Beloved SON, Who, in obedience to Thy Will, consummated His Life of toil and self-denial by the Death of the Cross. Can we then dare to shrink from our share of pain and humiliation? Enable us, we beseech Thee, O LORD, so to use the world as though we used it not, that we may offer ourselves to Thee, dead according to the flesh, but living with the Spirit of "CHRIST, Who is our Life" (Col. iii. 4).

Of Self-discipline.

THE EXERCISE OF THIS VIRTUE.

FIRST POINT.

LET us adore our LORD JESUS CHRIST, spending the whole course of His earthly Life in the denial and discipline of self. "CHRIST pleased not Himself" (Rom. xv. 3). He, although clothed with our flesh, was yet not subject to it, being ever guided by His own Divine SPIRIT He was "like as we are, yet without sin" (Heb. iv. 15). Nevertheless, in order that He might be our example in all things, and that we might be moved to gain the grace of self-discipline, He tells us, by His Prophet, that His Life was passed in suffering and privation: "I am afflicted and ready to die from My youth up" (Ps. lxxxviii. 15).

SECOND POINT.

A WELL-DISCIPLINED Christian strives without ceasing to conquer himself, and to rule every action of his life, whether great or small, in accordance with GOD'S holy Will.

For this end he is ready to undergo any suffering, and he willingly renounces even harmless and fully permitted recreations.

He deprives himself of all luxuries and superfluities. He uses the things of this world as though he used them not—employing them only in so far as they may be necessary for the life of the body, but not as deriving any gratification therefrom. And, lastly, he endeavours constantly to be conformed to the Spirit of CHRIST crucified, and in all privations and desolations he is never weary of contemplating the Cross of Calvary.

Let us examine whether we have not in many ways evaded this duty of self-discipline owing to our over-great tenderness and indulgence towards ourselves.

THIRD POINT.

O ALMIGHTY GOD, since the Christian's chief happiness is to follow in the footsteps of Thy Beloved SON, and since none can do so save by treading the path of self-discipline and self-denial, I will endeavour joyfully to exercise myself in these virtues. Give me the grace, O LORD, to remain constant in this resolution, and in order to this make me ever remember the saying which our Divine Redeemer Himself was pleased to leave for our instruction : " If any man will come after Me, let him deny himself, and take up his cross daily, and follow Me " (S. Luke ix. 23).

Of Self=discipline.

THE SUBDUAL OF OUR EVIL TEMPERS AND NATURAL INCLINATIONS.

FIRST POINT.

LET us adore the HOLY SPIRIT, Who, through the Apostle S. Paul, instructs us as to the necessity of subduing our evil tempers, and of disciplining our natural inclinations : " Let this mind be in you, which was also in CHRIST JESUS " (Phil. ii. 5). " If we live in the Spirit, let us also walk in the Spirit " (Gal. v. 25). In these precious sentences our Divine Master seems to say to us, " Rule your own spirits by entering into My SPIRIT, and by not pleasing your own selves." Is not this teaching worthy of the Teacher, and does it not claim our deepest and most reverential gratitude?

SECOND POINT.

LET us examine whether we have manfully warred with our evil tempers and inclinations—losing no opportunity of crushing and subduing them?

Do we not act very often from mere whim, with no other aim save that of indulging our own fancies and caprices?

Have we not sometimes omitted to do works of charity and devotion, only because we did not feel especially drawn towards them?

When we have been counselled to watch more diligently over ourselves, not to suffer ourselves to be carried away by outward distractions, and to live hardly, have we not rejected this advice because it was contrary to our inclinations? When we have been called upon to decide any important question, have we not consulted our own wishes rather than the Will of GOD?

Is not this habit of self-pleasing the cause of our unsteadfastness, and the want of exactness and of method in all which we undertake?

Lastly, do we not even yet seek to please ourselves in all things—in our friendships—our choice of work—our studies—our devotional readings; not selecting such as may profit us most, but only those which are most agreeable to us?

THIRD POINT.

O MY GOD, since our evil tempers and perverse inclinations are the chief cause of our frequent falls into sin, and since, if we are subject to them, we live, not as Christians, but like the heathen which know Thee not, I now resolve by the help of Thine all-powerful grace, to battle with them, to turn a deaf ear to all their temptations, and at once to cease from aught in which they have a part; for "we are debtors, not to the flesh to live after the flesh. For if ye live after the flesh, ye shall die; but if ye through the Spirit do mortify the deeds of the body, ye shall live. For as many as are led by the SPIRIT of GOD, they are the Sons of GOD" (Rom. viii. 12, 13, 14).

Of Self-discipline.

THE DISCIPLINE OF THE INTELLECT.

FIRST POINT.

LET us adore the HOLY SPIRIT, Who vouchsafeth to dwell in us to be the Fountain of our renewed life, and the Guide of all our actions. "Know ye not that ye are the temple of GOD, and that the SPIRIT of GOD dwelleth in you?" (1 Cor. iii. 16.) Since then this grace is given to us, should we not be blind indeed if we were to trust only to the light of our mere human reason? Let us shun this fatal error, and let us humbly implore the HOLY SPIRIT to preserve us from being thereby led astray.

SECOND POINT.

LET us examine whether we have strictly disciplined our reason and intellect, especially as regards the five points upon which we are most liable to be misled.

Firstly. Are we not often influenced by an overcurious and inquiring spirit—being always desirous, like the Athenians of old, "either to tell, or to hear some new thing" (Acts xvii. 21), or taking no pleasure save in out-of-the-way studies and researches, filling our minds with many vain and useless matters totally unconnected with our sacred calling?

Secondly. Do we war against the pride and conceit of human reason, which would fain persuade us to soar beyond our sphere by attempting to penetrate into the secrets of the Most High, and to grasp all the most incomprehensible mysteries of our holy Faith?

Thirdly. Do we strive to check within us the spirit of

frivolity and superficiality, by which the mind is kept in a perpetual state of hurry and excitement, so that we begin a meditation and never finish it—we take up one study and quickly throw it aside for another—we set about an employment, and then leave it for something else; and thus our time is wholly wasted in unprofitable labour?

Fourthly. Do we endeavour to moderate any excess of activity in the mind, causing us to bewilder ourselves with fruitless speculations, which disturb and unsettle us without leading to any satisfactory result?

Fifthly. Do we take all due care to avoid falling into the faults of obstinacy and self-sufficiency; and does it not often happen that what we, erroneously, term firmness, causes us to be unwilling to relinquish any opinion which we may have taken up—that we insist upon maintaining it at all costs—and that, after many contentions and disputes, grievously contrary to Christian charity, we at last are even led to question essential truths?

Let us now ask ourselves, what steps have we taken for our amendment upon these five heads?

THIRD POINT.

THE Saints of GOD have laid it down as an incontrovertible maxim, that no one can receive the HOLY SPIRIT until he has utterly annihilated the proud spirit of self within him. Can I then, O LORD, knowing this, refuse to subject my rebellious intellect to Thee? With my whole heart do I renounce this unworthy pride of human reason; and I beseech Thee, O my GOD, to grant me Thy grace that I may so humble myself as to be counted of the number of those happy souls whom S. Augustine thus apostrophizes: " Blessed are the poor in spirit "—that is to say, those who have laid aside the presumptuous spirit of self—" for they are rich in the gifts of the SPIRIT of GOD."

Of Self=discipline.

THE SUBDUAL OF THE LOVE OF SELF.

FIRST POINT.

LET us adore the HOLY SPIRIT, filling our hearts with His Divine Love in order to purify them from the love of self, and to inspire us with that hatred of ourselves to which our Blessed LORD exhorts us in the Gospel. "He that hateth his life in this world, shall keep it unto life eternal." (S. John xii. 25).

SECOND POINT.

THOSE who have not subdued in themselves the love of self, think only of passing through life with as little trouble and inconvenience as possible : they are ever careful of themselves, and they shun toil and anxiety : and they neglect the duties of their calling, readily allowing them to devolve upon whomsoever will undertake them.

They cannot endure the least hardness, or the want of any superfluity to which they may have accustomed themselves.

They make large demands upon the patience and forbearance of others ; but they are unable to sympathize with them in return, or to enter with interest into any matter which does not personally touch themselves : they choose their work to suit their own tastes, and they only value such exercises of devotion as they find to be easy and pleasant.

In short, from excess of self-love they neglect the work which GOD has given them to do, and the souls committed by Him to their charge : they become, as it were, their own idols, and thus they fall into those sins to which S. Paul alludes as the sad fruits of the love of self. "In the last days ..... men shall be lovers of their own selves, covetous, boasters, proud, ... unthankful, unholy ..... lovers of pleasures more than lovers of GOD" (2 Tim. iii. 1, 2. 4).

Let us now ask ourselves if we have made any progress in disciplining and subduing the love of self.

THIRD POINT.

O GOD of Love, it is by Thine All-powerful Love alone that the hateful love of self can be subdued and crushed. Come, then, O LORD, and let Thy Divine Love reign triumphantly in our hearts, and fill them with that celestial Fire which will utterly consume the very last remnants of self, leaving only the pure flame of the love of Thee.

EXAMEN PRO CLERO.

Of the Saintliness of Life required in the Priesthood.

FIRST POINT.

LET us adore the HOLY SPIRIT, Who watches with especial care over those who have been called to the Priesthood, to incline them to holiness of life. He urgently beseeches them, not only speaking to them Himself by the Holy Scriptures, but also through the writings of the Fathers, and the Councils of the Church, wherein no point is more frequently insisted upon than the obligation which all Priests are under, to strive after a more than common degree of holiness. Let us acknowledge humbly this Fatherly Goodness, and endeavour to respond to it by the strict fulfilment of all our duties.

SECOND POINT.

THE holiness necessary in the Priestly life requires, according to the Fathers and the Councils of the Church of GOD, that we should observe the following precepts :—

I. That we should strive to avoid, as far as may be, even the most venial sins.

II. That we should fly from all that bears the appearance of evil.

III. That we should be desirous of performing, by the Divine help, every good work.

IV. That we should seek to attain to an eminent degree of virtue.
V. That we should raise the level of that perfectness at which we aim as high as possible.

Let us test ourselves by these five rules, that so we may judge if we have tried to act up to them.

Firstly. Have we striven to avoid venial sins? Have we not rather, like the world in general, thought that holiness consisted simply in the avoidance of mortal sin? And, acting on this principle, have we not permitted ourselves to be inattentive at our devotions, listless in time of prayer, careless and irreverent during Divine Service? And have we not been too little anxious to refrain from opportunities which offer of indulging in frivolities, detraction, unnecessary talking, and many other venial sins?

Secondly. Have we abstained from even the shadow of evil—from idle conversations and amusements, from intimacies with worldly people, or with those members of the Church who do not live up to their profession—thus giving reason to suppose that our lives also are not in accordance with our rule?

Thirdly. Have we been ready and desirous to perform all good works—employing all our time diligently and well, faithfully fulfilling all our duties, and eagerly embracing all those opportunities of doing good which the Providence of GOD places before us, especially in such as belong more particularly to our state of life?

Fourthly. Have we endeavoured to acquire, in an eminent degree, all those virtues which have been most fully shown forth by the Saints of GOD—not contenting ourselves with approaching them in one or two points, but using every effort to keep a perfect image of them ever before our eyes?

Fifthly. Do we not set bounds to our aspirations after holiness, and do we not prescribe for ourselves certain devotional practices, beyond which we do not choose to go?—instead of seeking by GOD'S grace to advance farther and farther in the path of perfection; since not to make progress is to go back, and since it is of the nature of sin not to reach the highest point to which we can attain.

THIRD POINT.

O MY GOD, Thy Priests are set before Thy people for an example: they are constantly in Thy temple, and they minister at Thy Altar—nay, they offer the Holy Sacrifice of Thy most Precious Body and Blood, thus filling a higher office than even Thine Angels. O LORD, grant that we may fully realize the obligation imposed upon us by the possession of these inestimable privileges—that we should purify ourselves, even as Thou art pure.

Of being Called to the Priesthood.

FIRST POINT.

LET us adore our Great Example, the LORD JESUS CHRIST, Who, in order to set forth fully to all those entering into the Priesthood the necessity of a special vocation thereto, did not Himself—all-holy as He was, begin His work until He was called to it by His FATHER. " No man taketh this honour unto himself, but he that is called of GOD, as was Aaron. So also CHRIST glorified not Himself to be made an High Priest" (Heb. v. 4, 5). Let us then profit by this great Example, and humbly render thanks to the SON of GOD, Who deigns to set it before us.

SECOND POINT.

LET us examine whether we have not entered into Holy Orders without sufficiently seeking to know the Will of GOD concerning us.

Have we not decided upon embracing that state of life simply from our own wish or fancy—without taking any time to reflect—without imploring the guidance of the HOLY SPIRIT—or without passing, at least, a certain time in prayer and meditation?

Has not our choice been made from thoughtlessness and caprice, and have we not made up our minds too hastily—perhaps from false pride, not liking others to suppose that we had failed in what we had undertaken—perhaps from a morbid feeling of discontent, fearing that we should make a less brilliant figure in the world than we had hoped to do?

May we not, too, have been actuated by the desire of gratifying our relations—affection for them leading us to enter blindly into their schemes, which have, often, only our temporal advantage in view, and thus are opposed to the spirit of the Gospel?

May we not likewise have been influenced by delicacy of health, weakness of body, or inaptitude for secular employments?

Have we not been moved by ambition, and love of the outward grandeur of our office; or by covetousness, desiring to heap up riches; or by sloth, and dread of exertion, which makes us hope to enjoy in the Priesthood an easy, tranquil existence, in which we are well provided for, and are exempt from care and anxiety?

Have we not been so full of presumption as to imagine that our talents were such as to qualify us for the highest posts in the Church, and that we need not therefore question too closely the reality of our vocation?

Lastly, have we not reason to fear that we may be amongst those who, for their sins, have been raised to the Priesthood, but also for their own condemnation?

THIRD POINT.

O MY GOD, we should not, uninvited, presume to offer ourselves to take service in the housholds of the great ones of this earth, and yet we dare to enter Thy sanctuary without being called by Thee. Keep us, O LORD, in Thy mercy, from so grievous a sin: or, if we have been so unhappy as to fall into t, grant us, we beseech Thee, the grace of a sincere and life-long repentance.

Of the Signs of our Calling to the Priesthood.

FIRST POINT.

LET us adore our LORD JESUS CHRIST, exhorting us by the mouth of His Apostle to examine thoroughly into the reality of our vocation : " See your calling, brethren " (1 Cor. i. 26). By these words, says S. Bernard, He desires us to weigh well whether we are called by His HOLY SPIRIT to the Priesthood. Let us take this saying to heart, that so it may be profitable to us.

SECOND POINT.

WE must try ourselves by the six tests which the Saints of GOD have appointed, to prove whether our call to Holy Orders be a true one.

The *First* is, having preserved our Baptismal innocence, or having, as far as in us lies, atoned for its loss by a humble and sincere repentance. "Who shall ascend into the hill of the LORD? or who shall stand in His holy place? He that hath clean hands and a pure heart" (Ps. xxiv. 3, 4). Have we not entered upon this sacred calling after having lost the grace which Baptism bestows, or without having sought, by the Divine help, to make reparation for our sin—nay, perhaps, even yet being in a state of sin, slaves to our own evil inclinations?

The *Second* test is that of singleness of heart. Have we embraced our ministry in the same spirit of single-heartedness with which our LORD established it? Has our sole object been to promote our Master's glory—to win souls to Him—and to devote ourselves utterly to the service of His Church?

The *Third* test is that our entrance into Holy Orders should be ecclesiastically legal. Have we made use of no unlawful methods to procure our admission—such as interest, subserviency, or importunity?

The *Fourth* test is that of great aptness for performing all ecclesiastical functions. Have we tried to unite propriety, modesty, and reverence of demeanour, the outward marks of our calling, with holiness, firmness, prudence, and all those inward graces which GOD requires in those who would meetly serve His sanctuary?

The *Fifth* test is the possession of the Priestly spirit, which is shown by the honour in which we hold even the lowest ranks of the Ministry—by a genuine love for all the Church's offices, and by great zeal for the preservation of discipline, and for the due observance of all rules.

Have such been our feelings?

Lastly, the *Sixth* test is the decision of our Bishop, or whoever may be delegated in his place. Have we listened to him as the interpreter of the Divine Will regarding us, and as the messenger whom GOD has Himself appointed to declare that Will to us? Have we faithfully disclosed to him our inmost thoughts, since, without an exact knowledge of the state of our souls, it is impossible for him to judge of the reality of our vocation? Have we then diligently carried out whatever he may have required of us, and have we been careful to take no step without consulting him?

THIRD POINT.

O MY GOD, if there be one point above all others on which the strictest self-examination is necessary, it is when judging of our call to the Priesthood, to see if it be truly from Thee. There is no point upon which self-deception is more common, and upon that point may depend, under GOD, the salvation of ourselves and that of the people committed to our charge. Give us, O LORD, we pray Thee, Thy Grace, whereby we may be enabled to prove ourselves, so that, when tried by all those tests which Thy Saints of old have established, we may, through Thy mercy, find our " calling and election sure."

Of the Priestly Spirit.

FIRST POINT.

LET us adore the providence of the All-Wise GOD, Who never appoints to His servants any state of life without at the same time bestowing upon them the strength and grace which they need for the fulfilment of their duties. When He chose Bezaleel to make the Ark, He "filled him with the Spirit of GOD, in wisdom, and in understanding, and in knowledge, and in all manner of workmanship" (Exod. xxxi. 3). When He appointed Moses to be the leader of the children of Israel, He imparted to him His Spirit of wisdom and light; and when He sent His SON to save mankind, He gave that Divine SAVIOUR His Spirit of love, whereby our redemption was accomplished. "Behold Mine Elect, in whom My Soul delighteth: I have put My Spirit upon Him" (Isa. xlii. 1). And this Spirit He will bestow upon all Priests who are truly called to serve Him. Oh, what shall we "render unto the LORD for all His benefits" to us?

SECOND POINT.

THE gift of the Priestly spirit enables us to share more abundantly in the Spirit of our LORD JESUS CHRIST, the Great High Priest. This Spirit causes us highly to reverence our sacred calling, and makes us strive after the virtues more especially belonging thereunto: it gives us a great love for the duties of our office, and imparts the grace through which we discharge those duties in a fitting manner. By these tests let us examine whether we have received the gift of the Priestly spirit.

Firstly. Has that "mind been in" us "which was also in

CHRIST JESUS"? (Phil. ii. 5.) Have we, like our High Priest, been filled with the spirit of self-sacrifice—ready to give time, health, life itself, if needful, for the glory of GOD and the salvation of mankind?

Secondly. Have we duly reverenced the great dignity of our office, the highest and holiest on earth—wondering meanwhile at the favour which our LORD has shown us in calling us, unworthy as we are, to such honour—thanking and praising Him without ceasing, and having no greater fear than that of profaning the sanctity of our Ministry by leading self-indulgent or worldly lives?

Thirdly. Have we striven after those virtues which are most needed in our office—perfect faith, angelic purity, burning zeal for the glory of GOD and the salvation of souls, fervent attachment to the Church, and a special love of prayer, study, and work for souls?

Fourthly. Have we earnestly devoted ourselves to all the functions of the Ministry—always speaking of them reverently, and considering the due performance of them as a great privilege, whether in small and, apparently, insignificant details, or in the most important and august ceremonies?

Fifthly. Have we discharged these duties fittingly, or at least have we earnestly endeavoured to do so, diligently informing ourselves of all prescribed observances, assiduously practising them, never shrinking from any difficulties which may at first oppose us, and sparing no toil in our efforts to overcome them?

Lastly. Have we cast away the spirit of this world—that is to say the love of pleasures, honours, and riches—this worldly spirit being utterly incompatible with the spirit of the Priesthood? "Now we have received, not the spirit of the world, but the Spirit which is of GOD" (1 Cor. ii. 12).

THIRD POINT.

O MY GOD, in every state of life it is most necessary that we should have the spirit of our calling; but far greater is this necessity in the Priesthood, because of all states of life it is the holiest, because its mission is the most important, and its duties are the most difficult. Make us, O LORD, to feel the wretchedness of a Priest in whom this spirit is wanting, so that, if we have not yet received it, we may diligently seek it from Thee; and if it has been already vouchsafed to us, that we may have the grace to keep it, as the Apostle has commanded: Quench not the Spirit" (1 Thess. v. 19).

Of the Frame of Mind in which we should receive the Gift of Holy Orders.

FIRST POINT.

LET us adore our LORD JESUS CHRIST, speaking thus in His Gospel, "Which of you, having to build a tower, sitteth not down first, and counteth the cost, whether he hath sufficient to finish it?" Many of the Saints of GOD apply this saying of our LORD to those who present themselves for Ordination. "Beware," say they, "how you enter unthinkingly into so solemn an engagement: weigh well what you are about to undertake; and do not attempt what may be beyond your powers." This counsel is all-important, and we are bound to hearken to it, and to give thanks to the HOLY SPIRIT, speaking to us by His servants.

SECOND POINT.

LET us examine in what frame of mind we have prepared ourselves for Ordination. The Saints of GOD have given us three tests:—1. earnest and devout meditation beforehand; 2. a long period of self-probation; and 3. a confirming of ourselves, by GOD'S grace, in righteousness of life.

Firstly. Have we, before presenting ourselves for Ordination, seriously reflected upon the vast importance of the step which we are about to take, and upon the nature of the grace which we are to receive? Have we remembered that this grace is conferred upon us in virtue of a Sacrament which cannot be repeated, and that, consequently, we run the risk of altogether losing the grace unless we are in a fit frame of mind for the reception of the Sacrament? And have we therefore remembered that we were in peril of life-long misery if we entered upon

P

our Ministry without having thoroughly examined our vocation, our capacity, and our natural tendencies, under the advice of a prudent and experienced Director?

Secondly. Have we taken due time to consider all these points, and have we striven to avoid all self-deception? Have we not persuaded ourselves that a few days or weeks of preparation were amply sufficient? Have we diligently laboured to acquire those virtues which are most essential to our calling?

Thirdly. Have we not imagined that, if we have given up the world, we are fully prepared, however recent that renunciation may be; not remembering that the Apostle forbids the Ordination of a novice (1 Tim. iii. 6), which is expounded as signifying one who has newly entered upon the life of faith, or the life of grace? Are we, through the Divine Grace, so confirmed in virtue as to be able to withstand temptations, to vanquish our evil inclinations, and to feel armed against all dangers which may beset us in the course of fulfilling our various duties?

Lastly. Having devoted all our powers of mind and soul to the task of preparing ourselves for Holy Orders, are we ready to submit with patience and meekness if our spiritual superiors see fit to defer our Ordination, or to refuse it altogether?

THIRD POINT.

O THOU Great GOD, Who seest the fearful peril of those who dare to enter the Priesthood without due preparation, without having tested themselves to the uttermost, and without being firmly grounded in virtue; grant, we pray Thee, that we may never presume rashly to invade Thy sanctuary before the time which Thou hast Thyself appointed to us.

Of Administering the Holy Sacraments.

FIRST POINT.

LET us adore our LORD JESUS CHRIST, Who, having instituted the Sacraments of His Church to be perpetual fountains of grace to all His faithful people, has appointed His Priests to administer them as "stewards of the Mysteries of GOD." How great should be our gratitude to Him Who, in His boundless goodness, places so great a charge in our hands.

SECOND POINT.

LET us examine what has been our frame of mind and our behaviour regarding the administration of the Sacraments.

Have we considered it as one of our principal duties, and, indeed, as the chief privilege of our sacred Office?

Have we not persuaded ourselves that it only concerned those who had the cure of souls, and have we not therefore neglected it when we ourselves have not been holding any charge?

Before administering any of the Sacraments have we carefully read the rubrics, and studied all that relates to the due observance of ritual?

Have we also taken care to be thoroughly acquainted with the nature of the Sacraments, so as to be able to give instruction to those who may need it, and to answer any difficult or embarrassing questions, such as are often put to the clergy?

Have we previously used our utmost endeavours to purify our hearts before our Heavenly FATHER by, at least, making an act of contrition, lest we should risk the commission of sacrilege by administering the Sacraments while in a state of mortal sin?

Have we, with equal care, aimed at singleness of intention,

having none other but to obey our LORD JESUS CHRIST and His Church?

Have we offered up our intention at the throne of GOD, and, renouncing all self-seeking, have we asked of Him the grace of administering in a right spirit?

Have we not administered in haste and negligently, without due outward and inward reverence?

Lastly, after having administered the Sacraments, have we immediately knelt in prayer to thank our LORD for having made us the channels whereby He communicates His gifts to men—to ask His pardon for all our imperfections—and to beg that His grace may always accompany us, that so we may do all things in a manner worthy of His Divine Majesty?

THIRD POINT.

O MY GOD, if in the kingdoms of this world the administrator of the revenue occupies one of the highest and most responsible posts, what words can convey a fitting idea of the infinite importance attaching to the administration of Thy Sacraments—the treasures of Thy Church? How strict an account wilt Thou demand from Thy Priests to whom they have been entrusted, and with what fear should they read those words of the Gospel, "Render an account of thy stewardship" (S. Luke xvi. 2). Enable us by Thy grace, O LORD, so to live that all zeal, piety, humility, and exactness may be found in us, and that we may be numbered amongst those favoured and faithful Priests of whom the Apostle spoke, saying, "it is required in stewards, that a man be found faithful" (1 Cor. iv. 2).

Of the Preparation necessary to enable Priests worthily to Celebrate.

FIRST POINT.

LET us adore our LORD JESUS CHRIST preparing to offer upon Mount Calvary the Sacrifice of Himself which is mystically commemorated day by day upon our Altars. He withdrew Himself from the tumult of the world, He retired to the Garden of Olives, He even separated Himself, for a time, from His Apostles. Then was His sacred Heart filled to overflowing with abhorrence of sin, with thirst for the salvation of mankind, with the spirit of self-sacrifice, with zeal for His FATHER'S glory. How perfect an example does our Blessed SAVIOUR here give us of the preparation which we should make, to enable ourselves, by His grace, worthily to celebrate the Holy Sacrifice.

SECOND POINT.

LET us examine how we have prepared ourselves to celebrate.

Do we remember that, as the Blessed Sacrament is the most sacred, the most august office of GOD'S Church, so to celebrate it fittingly requires the most devout and careful preparation?

Do we prepare ourselves to celebrate it by the performance of some work of charity, and by keeping ourselves, as far as possible, aloof from all worldly business?

Do we, likewise, from our first rising in the morning, avoid, as much as we can, all conversation upon secular subjects which might tend to distract our thoughts from the great duty before us?

Do we, on entering the sacristy to vest ourselves, spend some time in meditation and prayer?

Do we, at the same time, take care to purify our hearts by making an act of contrition, and, if necessary, by approaching the tribunal of penance?

Are we fully persuaded that, in order to be in a proper frame of mind for the celebration of so great a mystery, it is requisite, not only to be free from all stain of mortal sin, but to be without the slightest inclination to venial sin?

Whilst putting on the Eucharistic Vestments, do we repeat the prayers prescribed by the Church, and are we careful to recite them in strict conformity with her spirit?

During this time, and whilst going to the Altar, do we keep a strict watch over our thoughts, our eyes, and our tongues?

Lastly, following the example of so many devout Priests and servants of GOD, do we endeavour, by the Divine grace, to perform every action of our lives in a devotional spirit, since every moment of a Priest's life should be in some sort a preparation for the celebration of the most adorable Sacrifice?

THIRD POINT.

O ALMIGHTY GOD, if the priests of Thy tabernacle were required so diligently to purify themselves before offering to Thee the sacrifices of the Covenant, with what care should the Priests of Thy Church prepare themselves to offer the Sacrifice of Thy dear SON'S most precious Body and Blood. A whole life-time would not be too long a period to devote to our preparation, were we permitted but to celebrate once in the course of our Priesthood. Since then, I, whom Thou hast called to be Thy Priest, am bound by my Ordination vow to offer before Thee the Holy Sacrifice, I can do no less than strive to spend my life in such a manner as, by Thy grace, to make my every thought, word, and deed, an act of consecration to Thee and to the service of Thine Altar [1].

---

[1] "In service o'er the Mystic Feast I stand;
 I cleanse Thy victim-flock, and bring them near
 In holiest wise, and by a bloodless Rite.

O fire of love ! O gushing fount of light !
(As best I know, who need Thy cleansing hand)
Dread office this, bemired souls to clear
Of their defilement, and again make bright."

J. H. NEWMAN.
From S. Gregory Nazianzen.

Of Divine Service.

HOW WE SHOULD PREPARE OURSELVES FOR CONDUCTING IT.

FIRST POINT.

LET us adore our LORD JESUS CHRIST, earnestly desiring to show forth the glory of His FATHER. Let us, with reverent love, contemplate the burning zeal with which He calls upon His children to join Him in praising and magnifying the Maker of all things. "O praise the LORD with me, and let us magnify His Name together" (Ps. xxxiv. 3). Let us humbly return thanks to Him Who has been pleased to call us to the Ministry, thereby placing the conduct of Divine Service in our hands. How great is the honour thus conferred upon us. How should we rejoice in that He has appointed us to proclaim His praises on earth, even as His Angels do before His face in heaven.

SECOND POINT.

LET us examine in what manner we have prepared ourselves for the celebration of Divine Service.

Have we, beforehand, endeavoured to realize, with a living faith, the Presence of GOD, and the infinite Majesty of Him with Whom we are about to plead, and to Whom we are to offer praise?

Have we striven to purify our hearts, by making an act of contrition, that so we may not be found deserving of that terrible rebuke of which the Psalmist speaks: "Unto the ungodly said GOD, Why dost thou preach My laws, and takest My covenant in thy mouth?" (Ps. l. 16.)

How we should prepare ourselves for conducting it.

Have we carefully sought to withdraw our minds from all outward influences, especially from any affairs in which we feel a more than common interest, and which would therefore be likely to make our thoughts wander from the sacred duties in which we are about to be engaged?

Have we previously retired for a short space of silent meditation—more especially if we have been recently occupied about any worldly business—so as to banish all disturbing ideas, and to prepare our hearts to receive the gifts of the HOLY SPIRIT?

Have we implored the grace of our LORD JESUS CHRIST, Who alone perfectly shows forth the praise of His FATHER, and have we united ourselves in spirit to His Universal Church, in the name of which we, however feebly, proclaim that praise to His people?

Have we been careful to place our intention in conformity with that of our LORD and of His Church; and have we always been solicitous that our intentions should be suitable to the needs of the times or of the circumstances under which the Providence of GOD has ordained us to live?

In order to bar our hearts against the intrusion of disturbing thoughts, have we dwelt upon some pious reflection calculated to inspire us with devotion?

Have we made ourselves thoroughly acquainted with all rubrical directions, so as to avoid the danger of pre-occupation as to externals?

THIRD POINT.

O MY GOD, how few are there who, when about to approach the princes and great ones of this world, do not carefully prepare for the interview with which they are to be honoured; yet how many there are amongst Thy Priests who come unprepared into Thy Presence, and minister in Thy Sanctuary. I am overwhelmed with shame and confusion, O LORD, when I call to remembrance how often I have been guilty in this wise. Pardon me, I beseech Thee, of Thine infinite mercy; grant me the grace of a sincere repentance; and to this end fill me

How we should prepare ourselves for conducting it.

with a true sense of the greatness of this sin of unpreparedness; and let me not forget these words of the Son of Sirach: " Before thou prayest, prepare thyself; and be not as one that tempteth the LORD " (Ecclus. xviii. 23).

Of Divine Service.

THE FRAME OF MIND IN WHICH WE SHOULD CELEBRATE IT.

FIRST POINT.

LET us adore our LORD JESUS CHRIST, Who alone perfectly showeth forth the praise of His FATHER. All the thanks and praises which we are enabled to render to GOD in His Church, are, as it were, but a few drops overflowing from the full stream of praise offered by the Divine SON, and it is only through Him that our homage can be made acceptable to the King of kings. Let us reverently contemplate the sacred Heart of JESUS, filled with love and worship in a degree which we can but faintly conceive. Oh how perfect is the Pattern set before us. How Divine an example does our Blessed LORD give to those who serve His Altars.

SECOND POINT.

LET us ask ourselves whether we habitually celebrate Divine Service in a fitting frame of mind, such as the Church of GOD requires of us—*worthily, attentively,* and *devoutly.*

Firstly. Do we endeavour to perform it *worthily,* remembering that we stand in the Presence of GOD Himself, and that it is to Him that the words which we utter are addressed?

Have we felt and acknowledged our inability to call upon His Name, save by the grace of His HOLY SPIRIT?

Have we been penetrated with reverence and awe at the thought of His infinite Majesty?

Secondly. In order that we may conduct Divine Service *attentively,* have we carefully sought to exclude from our minds all subjects calculated to disturb us, under whatever form they may present themselves?

Have we roused ourselves even from any devout meditation which may have been out of season, since, in that case, we have no more right to indulge in such than in wrong or foolish thoughts?

Have we, in accordance with the counsels of the Saints of GOD, endeavoured, whilst reciting the Psalms, to stir up in our own hearts the feelings of contrition or of thankfulness expressed by the Psalmist?

Or in the Lessons, have we filled our minds with thoughts of the greatness of GOD, or with reflections on the recorded events of our SAVIOUR'S Life?

And have we united ourselves in spirit with our Blessed LORD, beseeching Him to enable us to do, with Him, the Will of His Heavenly FATHER?

And then, *Thirdly*, have we gone through Divine Service *devoutly*, that is to say, *lovingly*, with our hearts overflowing with thankfulness as we think of the wonderful beauty and excellence of that Service; *fervently*, giving ourselves up to the influence of the HOLY SPIRIT, Who showers down His graces upon faithful souls; and *joyfully*, as knowing how great is the privilege which is vouchsafed to us, of offering a perpetual sacrifice of prayer and praise before our GOD?

THIRD POINT.

O ALMIGHTY GOD, Who in calling us to the Priesthood, hast appointed us to lay before Thee, in the name of Thy people, the homage due to Thine infinite Majesty; bless, we beseech Thee, the resolve which we make to fulfil this duty with as high a perfection as we can attain unto. Thy boundless Goodness has made us members of CHRIST in His Church: He will make good that which is wanting in us. Grant that we may be made partakers of His SPIRIT, that so He Himself in us may render Thee the praises which we owe to Thee, "That GOD in all things may be glorified through JESUS CHRIST" (1 S. Pet. iv. 11).

Of Divine Service.

THE OUTWARD DEMEANOUR WITH WHICH WE SHOULD CELEBRATE IT.

FIRST POINT.

LET us adore the dealings of our Divine LORD and Master with us in having committed to us the charge of ministering at His Altars. Let us look upon this as one of the most convincing proofs of His love for us. How wonderful is the privilege which we possess of speaking to our King in the name of His Spouse the Church. Happy indeed are those who correspond faithfully with the graces thus bestowed upon them: but most miserable are those who fling away such manifold treasures of grace.

SECOND POINT.

LET us examine whether in the celebration of Divine Service we have preserved all those outward forms of reverence which the Saints of GOD have recommended to be practised: and let us ask, have we performed the Service—1. *distinctly*, 2. in its *entirety*, 3. *devoutly*, 4. in an *orderly*, and 5. in a *decent* manner?

Firstly. Have we taken care to articulate distinctly, without undue haste, or affected slowness?

Secondly. Are we especially solicitous to preserve the integrity of the Service, neither omitting any portion, nor substituting one prayer for another?

Thirdly. Do we conduct the Service devoutly, that is to say, with all the humility and reverence which so holy a duty demands?

And, *Lastly*, are we careful that all should be done decently and in order; that is to say, that all Rubrics should be strictly observed, that the most rigid punctuality as to time should be maintained, and that our outward demeanour should be in keeping with the sacredness of our office, and of the place wherein we minister?

THIRD POINT.

O MY GOD, Thou hast shown us with what reverence we should regard even the external duties of our holy Religion; and Thou hast sent Thy HOLY SPIRIT upon Thy Church to preserve this reverential feeling. Grant, we beseech Thee, that the same HOLY SPIRIT may give us the grace to abide by all the rules which Thy Church prescribes, for His aid alone can make and keep us faithful to our duties.

Of the Ceremonies of the Church.

FIRST POINT.

LET us adore our LORD JESUS CHRIST, Who came upon earth to teach His Church how she should honour GOD by a perfect worship, that is to say, a worship both inwardly and outwardly perfect. He desires indeed that we should "worship Him in spirit and in truth" (S. John iv. 24). Yet does He wish us likewise to show forth visibly our love for Him, and our reverence for the wondrous mysteries of His Sacraments, to which we strive to give expression in the Ceremonies ordained in the Church's Ritual. Let us, then, always contemplate these Ceremonies with feelings of due regard, and let us endeavour to carry them out in a loving and faithful spirit.

SECOND POINT.

THOSE who reverence, as they ought, the Ceremonies of the Church's Ritual, are very careful to make themselves thoroughly acquainted with all observances connected therewith, and they strive to carry them out faithfully and devoutly. Let us examine ourselves by these tests as to our fulfilment of the rules which the Church prescribes for our guidance.

Firstly. Have we really taken care to be duly instructed in all matters which concern the celebration of Divine Service, and the administration of the Sacraments? Have we studied the Rubrics attentively, and have we been deterred by no false shame from consulting those who are more learned than ourselves on these points, and from laying our doubts and perplexities before them? Have we not tried to persuade ourselves that many of these outward Ceremonies unprofitably employed time which might be better spent?

Secondly. Have we endeavoured to fulfil all permitted observances in a spirit of faithfulness—omitting nothing, and strictly following the regulations of the Church as to times and seasons, in order fully to develope her teaching?

Thirdly. Have we done all things in a loving spirit—striving to show in our outward bearing the inward worship which fills our hearts, and trusting, by GOD'S Grace, to inspire the congregations committed to our charge with the same feelings of devotion? Have we not been too much occupied with the externals of Ceremonies, so as to be in danger, both of forgetting the inner meaning, of which they are but symbols, and of falling into formal and mechanical practices?

Or, *Lastly,* on the other hand, may we not have had too little regard for these observances, either from a groundless fear that they may tend to withdraw our minds from GOD, or from a belief that they are only suited to the poor and ignorant, who require that Religion should be impressed upon their senses by a gorgeous and striking ceremonial?

THIRD POINT.

O ETERNAL GOD, the sacrifices of the Old Law were but types and shadows of the Great Sacrifice by which the New Law was established, and which we still show forth upon Thine Altars: yet how strictly didst Thou require the observance of these typical Rites. How zealous should we then be in obeying the commands of the still holier law which Thou hast delivered to us. Oh, give us Thy Grace, that we may never offend against it.

Of Preaching.

FIRST POINT.

LET us adore our LORD JESUS CHRIST, Who chose preaching as one of His chief works on earth, thus vouchsafing Himself to be the pattern for those who are appointed to announce His Word. He first showed forth in His own Life that which He taught when He began to speak to the people; and He did not begin to instruct them until He received from His FATHER the visible sign of His mission, by the descent of the HOLY SPIRIT upon Him. He preached alike to poor and rich, to the smallest company and to the greatest multitude, in waste and solitary places, and in the crowded city; and He spoke always in the simplest and clearest language, seeking only to glorify His FATHER, and to save sinners. Let us with grateful love adore and praise our Divine Redeemer, Who has deigned to show us in Himself the perfect Model for all who are called to preach to His people.

SECOND POINT.

LET us ask ourselves whether we have faithfully acquitted ourselves of this duty of preaching.

Have we not undertaken it without due reflection, without having meditated upon it seriously, in the Presence of GOD, without having consulted our Director, or without being called to it by our spiritual Superiors?

Have we refrained from preaching until we have ourselves endeavoured to practise those virtues which we desire to set forth to our hearers?

Have we not sought for the applause of men, instead of glorifying GOD alone?

Have we not sometimes given a forced interpretation to the Holy Scriptures, expounding them according to our own views, without due reverence or discretion?

Have we preached simply, clearly, and practically?

Simply—not affecting a florid style of eloquence, which may please the ear, but which cannot touch and convert the heart?

Clearly—avoiding too much subtleness of thought, abstract reasoning, and speculative reflections, which only weary the listeners?

Practically—taking for our principal subject the great truths of religion, and treating them so as to bear upon and influence the daily lives of our hearers?

Have we not sometimes preached without having previously prepared our discourse, either because we disliked trouble, or from having too much confidence in our natural talents?

Have we not thought too much of the reception which our preaching has met with, and have we not been too much depressed by censure, or elated by praise, instead of referring all to GOD, and being contented with whatever He may appoint for us, so that it be to His glory?

Lastly, has our zeal been such as to make us preach as the Apostle would have us to do? "Preach the word; be instant in season, out of season; reprove, rebuke, exhort with all long-suffering and doctrine" (2 Tim. iv. 2).

THIRD POINT.

O MY GOD, how plainly do we see, by the fear which S. Paul showed lest while preaching to others, he himself should "become a castaway" (1 Cor. ix. 27), that this great duty involves us in much spiritual peril, and that preachers, however saintly their lives may be, need to keep a constant strict watch over themselves, as did the Apostle. Grant, O LORD, that we may have the grace to follow his example; and, that we may not neglect our own salvation whilst labouring for that of others, imprint in our minds, we beseech Thee, these words of the Gospel, "What is a man profited, if he gain the whole world, and lose his own soul?" (S. Matt. xvi. 26.)

Of Catechizing.

FIRST POINT.

LET us adore GOD, Who, by the mouth of His Prophet reproaches us with the neglect of His little ones, to whom He wills that we should break the bread of His Word by catechizing them, and instructing them in all things necessary to salvation. "The young children ask bread, and no man breaketh it unto them." Thus we see our LORD'S great love towards His children, and His desire that we should apply ourselves earnestly to train them in the way they should go. Let us, then, praise His infinite goodness and loving-kindness.

SECOND POINT.

LET us ask ourselves how we have discharged the duty of catechizing—that is, giving simple and familiar explanations to the young and ignorant of the most important points of Christian doctrine.

It is one of our most indispensable duties, yet we frequently omit it, or regard it with dislike, because there is nothing brilliant or attractive about it, because it is looked upon with contempt by worldly people, or because we are afraid of being sometimes at fault in the course of our instructions.

Firstly. Have we not likewise neglected it from a foolishly conceited idea of our own capacity, which makes us imagine that we are fitted for greater things, and that we need not stoop to such humble employments?

Secondly. When we have been called upon to instruct very ignorant, coarse, or ill-disposed persons, have we not sometimes shown impatience and want of temper, which may have repelled them, and prevented them from deriving any benefit from what they heard? Have we taken equal pains with all, and have we been especially careful to show no preference or favour to one more than to another?

Thirdly. Instead of confining our instructions to those things which are necessary to salvation, have we not entered into unnecessary speculations above the capacity of our hearers? And have we not sought to embellish our discourse with rhetorical ornaments, more fitting for an orator than for a catechizer?

Lastly. Have we displayed all the gentleness, patience, and impartiality, which this duty requires from us?

THIRD POINT.

O MY GOD, Who desirest the salvation of all men, and Who knowest how many are in peril thereof through lack of instruction in the knowledge of Thee; give us, we beseech Thee, a true love of this duty which Thy Divine SON deigned to take upon Himself, which His Disciples zealously performed, and which has always been regarded as one of the chief missions of Thy Church.

Of Priestly Studies.

THE HIGH ESTIMATION IN WHICH STUDY SHOULD BE HELD BY US.

FIRST POINT.

LET us adore the warnings of Divine Justice, which our LORD sets before those of His Priests who wilfully neglect the studies which are necessary in their calling. Let us hear what He saith to them by the mouth of His Prophet Hosea: "Because thou hast rejected knowledge, I also will reject thee, that thou shalt be no priest to Me" (Hos. iv. 6). We may well tremble at these words, but our fear must be that godly fear through which we "work out" our "salvation" (Phil. ii. 12).

SECOND POINT.

LET us now ask ourselves whether we have had a real love, and a due veneration for study.

Have we been fully persuaded that wilful ignorance, in those who have entered upon the holy calling of the Priesthood, is a defect for which, according to the Fathers of the Church, no amount of uncultivated talent can atone, which the Councils of the Church have pronounced to be a disqualification for Holy Orders, and which the Word of GOD Himself declares to be a sufficient cause for rejection, thus showing plainly how it should be shunned by us?

Have we remembered that since we, who are Priests, are the guardians of GOD'S Word, of His Doctrine, and of His Truth; and since we are the instructors of His people, therefore the knowledge of all things concerning Salvation is absolutely indispensable to us? "The Priest's lips should keep knowledge, and they should seek the law at his mouth: for he is the Messenger of the LORD" (Mal. ii. 7). This knowledge can only be attained by study: have we then applied ourselves, with all fitting zeal, courage, and perseverance, to acquire it?

Have we not presumptuously deluded ourselves into the belief that devotion alone would supply the place of knowledge, and that—although we had taken no pains to deserve it—the Divine Light would be communicated to us in all difficulties?

Does not our negligence in this respect arise from an erroneous notion, that it suffices for a Priest diligently to fulfil the round of his ecclesiastical functions—though, in point of fact, these form but a single section of his duties?

Have we reflected that, even in the performance of our purely Sacerdotal functions, want of necessary knowledge may cause us to commit most fatal and irreparable errors?

Is not our negligence caused by inaptitude for study, and by slothfulness of spirit, which occasions an unwillingness to make the mental effort necessary for the acquirement of knowledge?

Lastly, being convinced that this knowledge—which at once enables us to "give an answer to every man that asketh" us "a reason of the hope that is in" us (1 S. Pet. iii. 15)—is no less requisite in a Priest than holiness of life, have we shunned ignorance and sin with equal care, having our hearts full set upon attaining unto wisdom as well as acquiring sanctity?

THIRD POINT.

O MY GOD, Thou hast shown clearly how essential is knowledge to Thy Priests, whom Thou hast appointed to be the light of the Body of Thy Church: open Thou then, we beseech Thee, our eyes, that we may see the full importance of this truth, and make us to understand how impossible it is for us—save by a miracle—to acquit ourselves faithfully of our duties, unless we are so thoroughly rooted and grounded in the truths of our holy Faith which we hold, as to be in danger neither of losing ourselves, nor of misleading others: for Thou hast said, "If the blind lead the blind, both shall fall into the ditch" (S. Matt. xv. 14).

Of Priestly Studies.

THE RULES WHICH WE SHOULD OBSERVE IN OUR STUDIES.

FIRST POINT.

LET us adore the LORD our GOD, Who is the fulness of all knowledge, which His Grace will impart to us, if we seek it aright. " The LORD is a GOD of knowledge" (1 Sam. ii. 3), and " He teacheth man knowledge" (Ps. xciv. 10). Let us reverently listen to the promise which He gives by the mouth of His Prophet, to make His habitation with those who order well all their doings; amongst which, study, to Ecclesiastics, must always be one of the most important. " Make your ways and your doings good, and I will dwell with you" (Jer. vii. 3, Vulg.).

SECOND POINT.

LET us examine whether we have observed the three great rules, which the Saints of GOD have laid down for us to follow in our studies, in order that they may be pursued in a manner worthy of the Christian profession—as to the *method*, as to the *mode*, and as to the *object*.

Firstly. As to the *method*.

Have we been careful to begin by acquainting ourselves thoroughly with those things which are necessary to salvation? Have we not spent much time, and taken extreme pains, in striving to master the most subtle questions in Theology, whilst we were ignorant of some of the simplest elementary grounds of our Faith? And have we not thus been led to neglect self-rule, and to remain stationary, even if we have not retrograded, in the paths of holiness?

Secondly. As to the *mode.*

How have we applied ourselves to study? Have we not often gone to it unwillingly, giving ourselves up to a spirit of slothfulness and negligence? Have we not felt a secret satisfaction at any interruption, and have we not allowed ourselves to be discouraged by very trifling difficulties? On the other hand, may we not have been too eager in the acquisition of knowledge —either trying to grapple with several subjects at once, and thus having no time to make ourselves masters of any, or subtracting time from our more specially sacred duties, in order to devote it to study?

Thirdly. As to the *object.*

What have we proposed to ourselves in our studies? Instead of thinking only of the Glory of GOD, and the salvation of our souls, and of those which He has committed to our care, have we not chiefly aimed at gratifying our vanity, at making a name for ourselves, and at acquiring a reputation for great learning? Have we not also been actuated by motives of self-interest, hoping to obtain preferment, and to rise in the world by means of our scholarly fame?

Lastly. Have we not been of the number of those who study with the vain idea that it is given to them to know all things, and to penetrate the hidden secrets of the Most High; taking no heed of the warnings of the HOLY SPIRIT? "For men to search their own glory is not glory" (Prov. xxv. 27, Vulg.: "He that is a searcher of majesty shall be overwhelmed by glory").

THIRD POINT.

O MY GOD, we know full well that all knowledge which is not directed by the fear of Thee can never advance the cause of Thy Truth; pardon us, we beseech Thee, the little care which we have hitherto taken to apply ourselves holily and worthily to the acquirement of all godly learning. Henceforth we will strive—Thy Grace aiding us—to grow, like Thy Saints, in knowledge of Thee and in all heavenly Wisdom, that so our work may not be unsanctified; for, lacking sanctification, it can never be acceptable to Thee.

Of Priestly Studies.

RULES TO ENABLE US TO PURSUE OUR STUDIES IN A CHRISTIAN SPIRIT.

FIRST POINT.

LET us adore our LORD and Master JESUS CHRIST, Who knowing how necessary it would be for us, His Priests, to apply ourselves to study, vouchsafes to impart to us, by His Saints, rules whereby we are enabled to sanctify all knowledge to His Service, and thus are admitted to share in the treasures of Divine Wisdom and Grace which are in Him. Let us humbly and gratefully acknowledge His goodness, and strive to render Him our thanks.

SECOND POINT.

HAVE we faithfully observed the rules laid down by the Saints of GOD for the sanctification of our studies?

Firstly. Before beginning any study have we always knelt down in prayer to beg GOD to give us the light of His HOLY SPIRIT? Have we implored Him to direct us, and to save us from the errors to which our unaided intellects are prone, and which often are the cause of our receiving, as truth, that which is but specious falsehood? In order to remove all obstacles which might intercept the light of grace from us, have we renounced all our evil tempers and wayward inclinations, which blind and mislead us, and likewise all inordinate attachments to the things of this world, which tend to chain us down to earth? Have we endeavoured to attain singleness of intention—only desiring to study in obedience to the Divine Will, in order that we may thereby be better enabled to discharge our duties, and become more efficient labourers in the vineyard of the Church of GOD?

Secondly. Whilst we are studying, do we follow the practice of S. Augustine, who, to use his own words, kept himself spiritually prostrate at the Feet of His SAVIOUR, "JESUM quærens in libris," seeking Him in the book upon which he was employed? When we perceive ourselves to be either very slothful, or over-eager, in study, do we endeavour to conquer our indolence, or to moderate our ardour, by lifting up our hearts to GOD and making a short meditation upon His Holy Will? Do we submit to the toil of study in a spirit of penitence, and, when any difficulty presents itself to us, do we have recourse to prayer, though at the cost of a short interruption to our work?

Thirdly. On concluding any study, do we turn the subject-matter over and over again in our minds, remembering that we shall have to render an account of it to GOD? Do we give Him thanks for the lights which He has vouchsafed to us, and do we offer them up to Him, beseeching Him to withdraw them from us, rather than that we should ever be tempted to use them otherwise than for His glory?

THIRD POINT.

O LORD, Thou hast taught us by Thy Apostle, that "Knowledge puffeth up, but charity edifieth" (1 Cor. viii. 1). Grant me, I pray Thee, the grace of studying in a Christian spirit; so may all learning which I acquire serve only to increase my love for Thee; so may the perfectness of that love supply the imperfectness of my knowledge.

Of Pastoral Visits.

FIRST POINT.

LET us adore our LORD JESUS CHRIST, visiting His people at divers times and in sundry ways, and setting before us a perfect model whereby to regulate our conduct in our pastoral visitations. Our Blessed SAVIOUR visited all mankind collectively when He came down on earth in the great mystery of the Incarnation. "The Day-spring from on high hath visited us" (S. Luke i. 78). He visited them individually during His mortal life. "Zacchæus, to-day I must abide at thy house" (S. Luke xix. 5). He visits us daily, both collectively and individually, in the most Holy Sacrament of the Altar. "What is man, that Thou art mindful of him? and the son of man, that Thou visitest him?" (Ps. viii. 4.) These visits of our loving LORD were and ever are prompted by the desire of promoting His FATHER'S glory, and of saving man: this twofold charity was the motive principle which led Him to seek His people, as well as His final aim in so doing. "Blessed be the LORD GOD of Israel; for He hath visited and redeemed His people" (S. Luke i. 68). Let us adore Him, praise Him, and give Him thanks for this His great lovingkindness.

SECOND POINT.

LET us question ourselves as to the spirit in which we have visited those committed to our pastoral care.

Have we not made some visits to those amongst our parishioners who may be superior in education and position, chiefly with the view of keeping up our intercourse with the world, or of acquiring or retaining popularity, from the fear of being thought morose or over-strict, or from the wish to display our talents?

Have we not made visits from a spirit of inquisitiveness, and from a desire to hear news?

Have we not been actuated by interested motives—being most assiduous in visiting those who have it in their power to be of use to us, and to give us preferment?

Have we made these visits of duty a pretext for keeping up worldly intimacies?

If we have been careful to eradicate all traces of the above unworthy motives, have we with equal solicitude endeavoured, by the Divine Grace, to aim always at going through this part of our duties in a truly Christian spirit?

Have we unceasingly kept in view the glory of GOD, submission to the decrees of His Providence, and the fulfilling of His holy Will?

Have we sought to imitate the Apostle, who—ever remembering that, as he has himself told us, "we, being many, are one body in CHRIST, and every one members one of another" (Rom. xii. 5)—was always, in his ministrations amongst the people, "fervent in spirit, patient in tribulation—not" minding "high things, but" condescending "to men of low estate"?

Do we strive to inspire those committed to our charge with a detestation of sin, and to lead them upwards through reverence for Christian Truth to love of the Gospel of CHRIST, and to the practice of the precepts contained therein?

When our duty calls us to visit persons in affliction, do we go thither as to Calvary, honouring our suffering Redeemer in His Members?

If they are in poverty, do we feel that, in relieving them, we are ministering to our Blessed LORD Himself, as He has told us? (S. Matt. xxv. 40.)

If they are living under the yoke of sin, do we endeavour to free them from that bondage, and to lead them back to GOD, with all the loving tenderness which true charity inspires?

Lastly, in whatever visits we may have to make, do we try to enter into the spirit of our LORD and Master, and to unite ourselves in intention to Him, that so we may be enabled by His Grace to imitate Him?

THIRD POINT.

O Merciful Saviour, Thou didst visit lost man, to redeem him, and to glorify Thy Heavenly Father : how, then, with Thy Example before our eyes, can we, in our pastoral visits, be actuated by any lower motives than those of obeying Thee, and bringing our brethren into the way of salvation. This, O my God, shall henceforth, by the help of Thy Grace, be the aim of all my endeavours; that so, walking humbly in the path which Thou hast traced for me, I may be able to repeat Thy Divine words, "I am come that they might have life, and that they might have it more abundantly" (S. John x. 10).

Of the Good Example which Priests are bound to give.

FIRST POINT.

LET us adore our Blessed LORD, Who, having appointed the Priests of His Church to be the rule and model of Christian Life to all people, admonishes them in an especial manner, by the mouth of His Apostle, to remember this obligation which has been laid upon them. "In all things showing thyself a pattern of good works: in doctrine showing uncorruptness, gravity, sincerity" (Tit. ii. 7). "Be thou an example of the believers, in word, in conversation, in charity, in spirit, in faith, in purity" (1 S. Tim. iv. 12). Let us receive these exhortations in a spirit of docility, reverence, and gratitude, and let us strive to imprint them deeply in our hearts.

SECOND POINT.

LET us examine these instructions in detail, in order that we may see whether we have faithfully fulfilled the duty of giving a good example.

Firstly. Have we shown it in *doctrine* and in *word*, by our zeal in teaching a sound Christianity—labouring earnestly to instruct our people, maintaining every where the truths of the Gospel, and vigorously combating whatever tends to corrupt our holy Faith, and to relax Morality?

Secondly. Have we given good example in *conversation*—endeavouring, in our intercourse with others, to make all topics, directly or indirectly, a source of edification?

Thirdly. Do we show a good example in *gravity*—preserving always by our outward demeanour the dignity of our calling, although without assuming a repellant severity of manner?

Of the Good Example of Priests.

Fourthly. Do we show it in *charity*—by seeking in every way to do good to all, by checking all evil speaking, by bearing with the defects of our neighbour, by serving him in all his needs, by sympathizing with him in his joys and sorrows?

Fifthly. Do we set forth a good example in *faith*—that real, living faith which guides and enlightens us, which is fruitful in good works, and which acts only in accordance with the Will of GOD, as revealed in His Word?

Sixthly. Do we give a good example in purity—studying to maintain a conduct above reproach, and avoiding all temptation to lead easy and self-indulgent lives?

Lastly. Have we, GOD aiding us, so ruled ourselves as to be to the laity, as it were, a book wherein they may behold an exemplification of those precepts which we are appointed to set before them?

THIRD POINT.

O ALMIGHTY GOD, it has pleased Thee to place us in Thy Church to instruct and enlighten Thy people, and Thou hast raised us above others in order that we may edify them by proving living examples of faith and good works. "Ye are the light of the world. Let your light so shine before men, that they may see your good works, and glorify your FATHER Which is in Heaven" (S. Matt. v. 14. 16). Do Thou, we beseech Thee, enable us by Thy All-powerful Grace so to rule our lives that they may be, unto all, patterns of holiness, instructing those for whose souls we are answerable in the way of Eternal Life.

Of the Renewal of Baptismal Vows.

FIRST POINT.

LET us adore our GOD in the boundless graces and mercies which He bestows upon His faithful people in Baptism. In It they become His children, members of His Beloved SON, and temples of the HOLY GHOST; nor is this all: for He even deigns to require great things at their hands. He requires that they should die to themselves and to the world, and that they should give themselves to Him. How great a cause for joy is it to the renewed man to be enabled again and again to repeat those solemn Vows, and to claim his share in so glorious a heritage.

SECOND POINT.

LET us ask ourselves whether the little care which we have taken to keep our Baptismal vows be not, in itself, sufficient reason for renewing them?

Firstly. Have we not often proved unfaithful to our solemn engagement to renounce the world, the flesh, and the devil? Instead of waging unceasing warfare against them, have we not given ear to their temptations, sometimes even, unhappily, to the extent of yielding to them?

Secondly. Have we made a sincere renunciation of the pomps and vanities of the world? Have we not, rather, felt a secret longing to enjoy them, to obtain preferment, to possess wealth, and to be held in honour by our fellow-creatures? And have we not given way to thoughts of ambition, arrogance, and self-complacency?

Thirdly. Have we steadfastly renounced all the works of the Evil One, as we promised in our Baptism? Have we not, on the contrary, suffered the old man to revive in us, and instead of stifling him at once, have we not fostered him in our bosoms, and thus risked the loss of the precious pearl of Baptismal Grace? Have we not been ashamed of the Gospel of CHRIST —shrinking from the upholding of His Name before the world, instead of maintaining the faith delivered to us, as the Priests of His Church are bound to do, at the risk of losing our worldly subsistence, our reputation, our very life?

Fourthly. Have we shown forth, by our lives, the reality of our Baptismal vows, and have we ratified them not only in word but in deed? "Not with our voices, but in our bearing; not with our tongues, but in our actions; not pronouncing them with our lips, but proclaiming them by our works," as S. Augustine says.

THIRD POINT.

O ALL-MERCIFUL GOD, Who, ever faithful to Thy promise, hast delivered me by Baptism from the slavery of sin, and hast made me to enjoy "the liberty wherewith CHRIST hath made us free" (Gal. v. 1), how am I covered with shame and confusion when I remember the little care which I have taken to keep my vows made to Thee. Help me now, I pray Thee, in the resolution which I make to return thanks each day that I live for the grace conferred upon me in Baptism, to renew my vows at stated times, and to keep them inviolate till my death. May the blessed anniversary of my admission into Thy Church, when, like Thy people of old, I was freed from bondage by passing through the waters, be ever to me a day of sacred joy and thanksgiving. "This day shall be unto you for a memorial; and ye shall keep it a feast to the LORD." "Remember this day, in which ye came out of Egypt, out of the house of bondage" (Exod. xii. 14; xiii. 3).

Of the Spirit of the World.

THE SIGNS OF THIS WORLDLY SPIRIT.

FIRST POINT.

LET us adore our LORD JESUS CHRIST, Who, teaching us by the mouth of His Apostle, that "we have received not the spirit of the world, but the Spirit which is of GOD" (1 Cor. ii. 12), shows us plainly thereby how far asunder are these two, and how completely we must cast aside the worldly spirit, if we would be filled with the Spirit of our Blessed SAVIOUR. Let us give thanks to Him for vouchsafing this instruction to us.

SECOND POINT.

THE Spirit of the World is entirely opposed to the Gospel of our LORD JESUS CHRIST, and wholly corrupt and sinful. "The whole world lieth in wickedness" (1 S. John v. 19). Let us now see whether we are ourselves infected therewith, or whether as Priests of the Church of GOD we withstand the Spirit of the World. And this we may know by the following signs.

Firstly. The Spirit of the World leads those who are possessed by it to love all things pertaining to the world, such as wealth, rank, splendid habitations, luxurious dress and furniture, varied amusements, and similar vanities which worldlings usually hold in high esteem. "Love not the world, neither the things that are in the world" (1 S. John ii. 15).

Secondly. The Spirit of the World prompts those who are enthralled by it to think and talk much of worldly matters; it makes them desirous to know what goes on in the world, and to be hearers and retailers of news. "They are of the world; therefore speak they of the world, and the world heareth them" (1 S. John iv. 5).

Thirdly. The Spirit of the World also makes us eager to please men, and to gain their approbation. We should remember how incompatible are these feelings with the love of GOD, and the desire of serving Him. "If I yet pleased men, I should not be the servant of CHRIST" (Gal. i. 10). "Know ye not that the friendship of the world is enmity with GOD? Whosoever therefore will be a friend of the world is the enemy of GOD" (S. James iv. 4).

Fourthly. Again; the Spirit of the World inclines us to conform ourselves entirely to the opinions and customs which happen to be in vogue, and to rule our lives by worldly precedents; all this being in direct opposition to the express admonition of the Apostle: "Be not conformed to this world" (Rom. xii. 2).

Lastly. Those who are in bondage to this Spirit are so blinded, that, in the service of the World, they willingly sacrifice their health, their peace of mind, their very existence; whilst in the service of GOD they are cold and apathetic, caring nothing for their own souls, or for the salvation of those for whom they are answerable to their Master. "The bewitching of naughtiness .... doth undermine the simple mind" (Wisd. iv. 12).

THIRD POINT.

O DIVINE REDEEMER, Thou hast Thyself taught us that Thy Spirit and the Spirit of the World are each so contrary to the other that there can be no accordance between them. "The Spirit of Truth, Whom the world cannot receive, because it seeth Him not, neither knoweth Him" (S. John xiv. 17). Deliver us, we beseech Thee, from that evil worldly Spirit, and strengthen us with Thy perfect Spirit, whereby our lives henceforth may be wholly ordered and governed.

Of the Spirit of the World.

OF THE WARFARE WHICH PRIESTS ARE BOUND TO MAINTAIN AGAINST THE WORLD.

FIRST POINT.

LET us adore our LORD JESUS CHRIST, keeping wholly apart from the World with which He had nothing in common. Let us here recall the fact that, on the very eve of His bitter Passion and Death, when He was about to be the Victim for the Redemption of all, He appeared to exclude the World from sharing in His Prayers, "I pray not for the World" (S. John xvii. 9), as though to mark forcibly how displeasing the world, and the spirit thereof, were, and are, to Him. Praise and blessing be to Him for ever, for thus giving us the example of renouncing all fellowship with the World.

SECOND POINT.

LET us examine how we have maintained our warfare with the World, especially as servants of the LORD JESUS CHRIST, and Priests of His Church.

Have we felt that aversion from the World which our LORD requires from us if we would be truly His Disciples?

Have we looked upon it as the greatest enemy of our holy Religion, as the opponent of our Divine Master, ever crying out by the mouth of its followers, "We will not have this Man to reign over us"? (S. Luke xix. 14.)

Have we always and in every way opposed ourselves to the World, endeavouring to win over those who are in its ranks to serve under the banner of CHRIST?

Have we loved and esteemed all which the World hates and despises, shunning what it seeks, and seeking what it rejects?

Have we remembered the solemn renunciation which we made, in our Baptismal vows, of the pomps and vanities of the World?

Have we, as far as possible, withdrawn ourselves from worldly society which the Saints of GOD have pronounced to be dangerous for all persons, but more especially so for Ecclesiastics?

In order that our separation from the world should be as complete as our holy calling requires it to be, have we, from our hearts, desired that it should be with us as the Apostle saith, "The World is crucified unto me, and I unto the World"? (Gal. vi. 14.)

THIRD POINT.

O ALMIGHTY GOD, when I consider how great are the woes pronounced by Thee against Babylon, which Thou didst swear to destroy in Thy wrath, I see plainly that it behoveth me utterly to renounce and reject the World; for, as the Fathers of Thy Church have interpreted, it is the World which is signified under the name of Babylon. Through Thy grace, O my GOD, may these reflections so wholly engross my mind as to lead me, ere it is too late, to take to myself the warning which Thy Prophet has given. "Flee out of the midst of Babylon, and deliver every man his soul" (Jer. li. 6).

Of Obedience.

THE REVERENCE AND LOVE PRIESTS SHOULD FEEL FOR THIS VIRTUE.

FIRST POINT.

LET us adore our LORD JESUS CHRIST, Who, in the fulness of His love of Obedience, came down from Heaven to do His FATHER'S Will, and in doing it found His chief delight and sustenance. "Lo, I come to do Thy Will, O GOD" (Heb. x. 9). "My meat is to do the Will of Him that sent Me" (S. John iv. 34). That Will was a law to Him, even unto death. "Even so, FATHER, for so it seemed good in Thy sight" (S. Matt. xi. 26). Does not this prove to us how dear and precious was the virtue of obedience to Him?

SECOND POINT.

LET us examine whether we, who should be examples to the flock of GOD, as His Priests, have felt for this great and essential virtue all the love and reverence which it claims from us.

Have we believed with the Saints of GOD that obedience is in itself the epitome of all other virtues, and that, as S. Augustine says, it is the Foundation, the Mother, and the Guardian of them all?

Do we believe that obedience is the one sure path—the royal road which CHRIST Himself has traced for us, and out of which no safety is to be found? "He became the Author of eternal Salvation unto all them that obey Him" (Heb. v. 9).

Do we remember that he who is truly obedient possesses himself in perfect peace and strength, satisfied with whatever the Will of God may appoint for him? "Great is the peace that they have who love Thy law; and they are not offended at it" (Ps. cxix. 165).

And do we remember how closely this virtue unites us to our Blessed LORD—even as He Himself hath told us, by the strongest and most tender of ties? "Whosoever shall do the Will of My FATHER which is in Heaven, the same is My brother, and sister, and mother" (S. Matt. xii. 50).

Do we firmly believe that obedience is of absolute necessity to all; and that, since our SAVIOUR, the Great High Priest, has Himself given us the example thereof, we who are His Priests, are more especially bound to claim no exemption?

And are we fully convinced that no prayers, or almsdeeds, or acts of self-denial can be acceptable in the sight of God, except they are undertaken in the spirit of obedience to His holy Will?

We have our Divine Redeemer's own Words to assure us of the great reward promised to the obedient. "Not every one that saith unto Me, LORD, LORD, shall enter into the Kingdom of Heaven; but he that doeth the Will of My FATHER which is in Heaven" (S. Matt. vii. 21). It was this which caused S. Bernard to make use of the following forcible and well-known expression, in his Sermon on the Resurrection: "Could the spirit of disobedience and self-will be rooted out, Hell itself would exist no longer."

THIRD POINT.

O ALMIGHTY GOD, it was in the spirit of obedience that Thy Beloved SON came down from Heaven to redeem us by His Blood; "I seek not Mine own Will, but the Will of the FATHER which hath sent Me" (S. John v. 30). Hence we learn that our LORD had even, as it were, a special love of this virtue, whereof He gave so wondrous an example. Enable me, I beseech Thee, O my GOD, so to become imbued with the same spirit of obedience, that I may ever offer to Thee that sacrifice which Thou hast declared to be more acceptable to Thee than burnt offerings—even the sacrifice of my own will. "Behold, to obey is better than sacrifice, and to hearken than the fat of rams" (1 Sam. xv. 22).

Of Obedience.

THE PRACTICE OF THIS VIRTUE.

FIRST POINT.

LET us adore our LORD JESUS CHRIST, teaching us by His example to obey always and in all things. "The FATHER hath not left Me alone: for I do always those things that please Him" (S. John viii. 29). And not only did He obey His Heavenly FATHER, the King of Kings, and LORD of Lords, but He vouchsafed to be obedient to His Mother, the Blessed Virgin, and to His foster-father, S. Joseph. "He went down with them, and came to Nazareth, and was subject unto them" (S. Luke ii. 51). Let us then give thanks to Him for having thus shown us a perfect pattern of obedience, in order to inspire us with the love of this virtue, whereby we may be enabled to walk in the way of salvation.

SECOND POINT.

THOSE who are thoroughly imbued with the spirit of Obedience eagerly seek and promptly embrace opportunities for the submission of their own wills.

They prefer a subordinate position to one in which they are obliged to take the lead; and if they accept a post of command, they only do so in obedience to the orders of their ecclesiastical superiors.

They are careful not to live without a rule, feeling that it is a serious fault not to portion out the day systematically, so as to give to each hour its appointed task. If they are in sole charge of a cure, and are thus, in a measure, left to their own guidance, they all the more strictly observe this rule, and they strive by every means to subdue their own wills and to practise obedience.

If they are members of a capitular or collegiate body, they remember that they owe to their Ecclesiastical superiors the same obedience which is due from a child to his parents, and they refrain from all complaining, and from murmuring against them, however irksome and severe the orders issued by them may appear to be.

Lastly, to such as are here described nothing is more abhorrent than the sin of disobedience, which they justly consider as one of the most deadly poisons of the soul. "Rebellion is as the sin of witchcraft, and stubbornness is as iniquity and idolatry" (1 Sam. xv. 23).

Let us now ask ourselves whether we have faithfully practised this virtue of obedience.

THIRD POINT.

O MY GOD, how can we refuse to obey our fellow-creatures for the love of Thee, when Thy dear SON Himself did not disdain to obey His creatures for the love of us? By Thy grace I now resolve to live and die in the practice of this virtue. Bless, O LORD, I beseech Thee, this resolution, that so I may persevere unto the end, and thus be preserved from the peril of losing Thy grace by departing from obedience: for, as has been said by a great master of the spiritual life—the author of the "Imitation of CHRIST"—" He who striveth to withdraw himself from obedience withdraweth himself from grace."

Viri Venerabiles.

MEN of reverend estate, Priests of GOD Eternal,
Heralds of the LORD most High, lamps of day supernal,
Burning with the fire of love, bright with hope's reflection,
Words of counsel from my mouth take for your direction.

GOD to serve within His Courts, to your lot it falleth;
CHRIST, the true, unfading Vine, you His branches calleth;
See ye be not barren found, or leaves only bearing,
If the life of the true Stem ye have hope of sharing.

Of the Law of Catholics ye are sworn defenders,
Salt to earth, the light of men, of CHRIST'S flock the tenders;
Walls are ye to Israel, godly manners preaching;
Judges in the Church of GOD, divers nations teaching.

Soon the Law itself will fall, if its guardians waver;
"If the salt his saltness lose, what shall give it savour?"
If the light shall cease to shine, soon the way is quitted;
If the shepherd fail to watch, inroads are committed.

Ye the vineyard of the LORD hold for cultivation;
Streams of doctrine ye must pour for its irrigation:
Thorns and thistles ye must slay, noisome weeds uprooting,
That the plant of faith may grow, ever freshly shooting.

Oxen in the threshing-floor, ye are personating;
Grain, which from the chaff ye tread, wisely separating:
Of the Law the laity hold you for a mirror;
Frail are they and wavering, prone full oft to error.

Whatsoever they behold you with anger viewing,
That the laity are found carefully eschewing,
Whatsoever they observe you in deed fulfilling,
That they lawful deem, and walk in your steps right willing.

Since then ye are shepherds made, bound the sheep to number,
Be ye not as idle dogs, dumb and prone to slumber,
Let the sound of your shrill bark still the envious howling
Of the wolves which, bent on prey, round the fold are prowling.

Threefold bread the faithful flock needs for sustentation ;
First, the Body of the LORD, for the soul's salvation,
Then, the seed of heavenly truth, wisely sown in meekness :
Lastly, food of earthly growth, for the body's weakness.

To your sheep to speak the word ye are bounden therefore ;
But to whom, how, what, and where ; when, how long, and wherefore ;
On these points ye ought to spend much deliberation,
Lest ye should be found at fault in this ministration.

To the duty it pertains of your high commission
To dispense the gifts of grace freely on petition ;
But should ye the boon of faith be for profit vending,
Know Gehazi's leprosy is o'er you impending.

Freely of the Eucharist offer distribution ;
Baptism freely ye must give, freely Absolution ;
Freely ye have all received ; free be all your giving ;
Only that which was your own save to be your living.

Let Religion in your walk find her meet expression,
Keep your conscience clear, your life free from all transgression :
Be your guise canonical, fair your reputation ;
Let no criminous offence blot your estimation.

See no arrogance of soul mar your inward fitness ;
Let your dress and aspect grave render faithful witness ;
Nought should by degrading cares work your souls' ensnaring,
Who the heavenly kingdom's keys in your hands are bearing.

Let your words be short and few, lest much conversation,
Nurse of every vanity, lead to condemnation;
Let your brevity of speech guard you from this danger;
For " in multitude of words sin is not a stranger."

Be ye sober, peaceable, kind, discreet in daring;
Simple, chaste, compassionate, upright and forbearing,
Hospitable, pious, meek; well your flock advising;
Giving comfort to the sad, evil men chastising.

Oh, may ye the shepherd's heart in your cures inherit,
And throughout your earthly life walk as in the Spirit;
So that when this garb of flesh ye aside are casting,
From the LORD ye may receive vestures everlasting.

H. R. B.

BY THE SAME EDITOR.

THE ASCETIC LIBRARY : *A Series of Translations, from Catholic Sources, of books for devotional reading.*
   I. MYSTERIES OF MOUNT CALVARY: *Meditations on the Passion.* From the Latin. 3s. 6d.
   II. PREPARATION FOR DEATH. *Meditations for Advent.* From the Italian. 5s.
   III. COUNSELS ON HOLINESS OF LIFE. From the Spanish. 5s.
   IV. EXAMINATION OF CONSCIENCE, ON SPECIAL SUBJECTS. From the French. 5s.
   To be followed by other Works in Preparation.

In the Press, by various Writers, in crown 8vo,
A GLOSSARY OF ECCLESIASTICAL TERMS : Containing Explanations of Terms used in Architecture, Ecclesiology, Hymnology, Law, Ritualism, Theology, Heresies, and Miscellaneous Subjects.

SIX SHORT SERMONS ON SIN : Lent Lectures at S. Alban-the-Martyr, Holborn, 1867. Fourth Thousand. 1s.
   1. The Nature of Sin.
   2. The Effect of Sin.
   3. The Remedy for Sin.
   4. The Knowledge of Sin.
   5. The Removal of Sin.
   6. Holiness after Sin.

RIVINGTONS, LONDON, OXFORD, AND CAMBRIDGE.

THE RITUAL OF THE ALTAR: *Containing the Office of Holy Communion, Rubrical Directions, Private Prayers in Latin and English, and Ritual Music, according to the Use of the Church of England: together with Directions for the Sacred Ministers and Assistants, the Preparation and Thanksgiving, various Collects, Epistles, and Gospels, and an Appendix of General Rubrics.* [Nearly ready.

BOURDALOUE : *Spiritual Exercises;* Readings for a Retreat. From the French. 2s. 6d.

THE DAILY SACRIFICE : *A Manual of Spiritual Communion.* Fifth Thousand. 1s. 3d. and 1s. 9d.

THE DIVINE LITURGY : *A Manual for the Sacrament of the Altar.* Ninth Thousand. 1s., 1s. 6d., and 2s. 6d.

THE LITURGIES OF 1549 AND 1662. The Office of Holy Communion of the First Book of Edward VI., and of our own Prayer Book, printed in parallel pages. 2s. 6d.

AVRILLON : *On the Holy Spirit;* Readings for Ascension and Whitsuntide. From the French. 2s.

LUIS DE GRANADA : *Considerations on Death, Judgment, Heaven, Hell, &c.* From the Spanish. 3s.

MASTERS, ALDERSGATE STREET, AND NEW BOND STREET.

BY THE SAME EDITOR.

AVRILLON: *Eucharistic Meditations for a Month.* From the French. 4s.

RODRIGUEZ: *On the Virtue of Humility.* From the Spanish. 2s.

SHORT DAILY MEDITATIONS FOR A MONTH. 2s.

SHORT DAILY MEDITATIONS FOR THE SEASONS. From Advent to Easter. 2s. 6d.

EUCHARISTIC LITANIES. 2s. 6d.

ORDER OF UNCTION. *After the use of Sarum.* 3d.

MASTERS, ALDERSGATE STREET, AND NEW BOND STREET.

Lately published, cloth extra, with facsimiles of 5 original Woodcuts, 10s. 6d.,
THE FEMALL GLORY : *The Life and Death of our Blessed Lady, the Holy Virgin Mary, God's Own Immaculate Mother.* By ANTHONY STAFFORD. Together with a new Preface ; the Apology of the Author ; and an Essay on the Cultus of the Blessed Virgin, by an Anglican Priest.

Lately published, 3s. 6d.,
INVOCATION OF SAINTS AND ANGELS. *Compiled from Greek, English, and Latin Sources, for the Use of Members of the Church of England.*

In the Press, uniform with Invocation of Saints,
SPIRITUAL EXERCISES OF S. IGNATIUS. *Newly Translated from the Original.*

In One Volume, 9s. 6d., *or in Nine Numbers,*
TRACTS FOR THE DAY : *Essays on Theological Subjects.* By various Authors.

Uniform, 15s. *each, cloth,*
THE CHURCH AND THE WORLD : *Essays on Questions of the Day.* By various Writers.
    First Volume of the Series. 1866. *Third Edition.*
    Second Volume of the Series. 1867. *Second Edition.*
    Third Volume of the Series. 1868.

Uniform, toned paper, limp cloth, red edges, 5s.,
HYMNS AND VERSES, ANCIENT AND MODERN :—
    I. LYRA MESSIANICA : *On the Life of Christ.* Second Edition.
    II. LYRA EUCHARISTICA : *On the Holy Communion.* Second Edition.
    III. LYRA MYSTICA : *On Sacred Subjects.*

LONGMANS, GREEN, & CO., PATERNOSTER ROW.

Crown 8vo, price 7s. 6d.

DEVOTIONAL COMMENTARY

ON THE GOSPEL ACCORDING TO

S. Matthew.

Translated from the French of PASQUIER QUESNEL.

"A revised translation of Quesnel's 'Devotional Commentary' will be continued so as to include the further portions of Quesnel's excellent work, if the present volume is welcomed. Quesnel was one of those Gallicans who in the tone and doctrine of their devotional works approached very nearly indeed to the best of our own Church."—*Guardian.*

"Its object is to give 'the spiritual sense' of Holy Scripture, and this object is admirably carried out. We are glad to be able to give it our hearty and unqualified approval."—*John Bull.*

"It is a very acceptable manual for the religious, and its simple and practical character may be gleaned from the following comment."—*The Rock.*

"We can hardly give him (Pasquier Quesnel) higher praise than to say that he reminds us in many ways of the author of the 'Imitation.'"—*Clerical Journal.*

"The want which many devout persons feel for a commentary on the Scriptures with individual, practical, and devotional application, can hardly be better satisfied than by that of Quesnel." —*Church News.*

"It is exceedingly well done, and there is no occasion whatever for the translator to withhold his name."—*Churchman's Shilling Magazine.*

"The comments are brief, but pointed; and there is much to profit the reader by showing him what a depth of spiritual wisdom is treasured up even in the simplest utterances of our Lord."—*English Independent.*

"The commentary is eminently spiritual, and abounds in holy thoughts. Preachers will find abundance of material from it, and for home reading by private persons the book will, in its present dress, be accepted as a boon."—*Church Times.*

"We are glad to welcome this excellent new edition of our old friend Quesnel on S. Matthew, which has not been published in England for a long time."—*Literary Churchman.*

"The commentary, we need scarcely say, is characterized by true fervency, and humility of devotion, the earnest breathings of a most sincere believer in an eternal, electing love."—*Record.*

"Generally speaking, we can give but a very qualified approval to the adaptations which make Romanist works suitable for purposes of Protestant edification. If an exception were allowable, it would be in the case of Quesnel's 'Reflections,' a book which has a more striking history than any other of the same class."—*London Quarterly Review.*

"This carefully and handsomely produced version of the first portion of the commentaries of Quesnel may be taken, we conceive, as evidence of the tendency which is so much to the credit of the Anglican or so-called Catholic Churchmen of this country—the tendency to bring the religious thought of England into harmony with the general religious thought of Europe. All persons to whom devotional commentaries on the Bible can be helpful as a mental or spiritual succour, and many persons to whom they can only be interesting as mental and spiritual facts, may read with advantage the meditations of this staunch and pious Frenchman, who carried down into a later generation the spirit and the sufferings of Arnauld and Nicole."—*Pall Mall Gazette.*

RIVINGTONS, LONDON, OXFORD, AND CAMBRIDGE.

Preparing for Publication.

Readings from the Spiritual Homilies of

S. MACARIUS;

FORMING A NEW VOLUME OF THE

Ascetic Library.

RIVINGTONS, LONDON, OXFORD, AND CAMBRIDGE.

www.ingramcontent.com/pod-product-compliance
Lightning Source LLC
Chambersburg PA
CBHW031950230426

43672CB00010B/2107